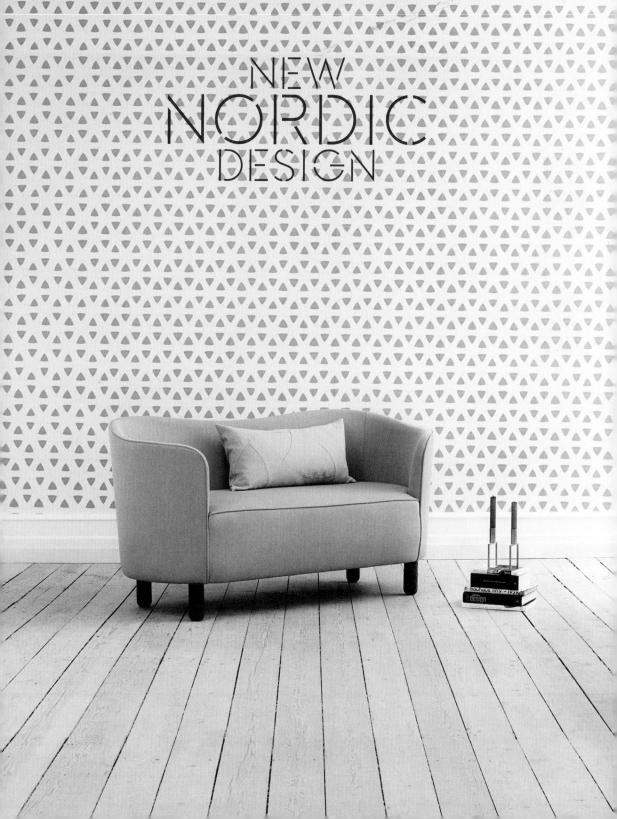

NEW NORDIC DESIGN

Thames & Hudson

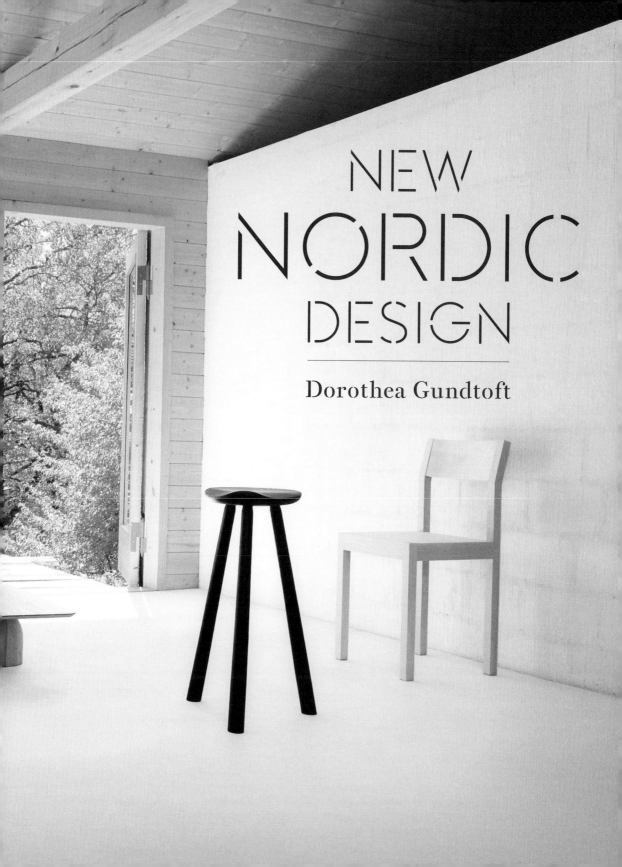

NEW
NORDIC
DESIGN

Dorothea Gundtoft

p. 1: 'Mingle' sofa, 1935, Flemming Lassen
pp. 2–3: Furniture designs, Nikari
below: 'Maya' tables, Beller

First published in the United Kingdom
in 2015 by Thames & Hudson Ltd,
181A High Holborn, London WC1V 7QX

New Nordic Design © 2015
Thames & Hudson Ltd, London
Text © 2015 Dorothea Gundtoft

Designed by Anna Perotti,
www.bytheskydesign.com

British Library Cataloguing-in-Publication
Data A catalogue record for this book is
available from the British Library

ISBN 978-0-500-51813-7

Printed and bound in China by
Toppan Leefung Printing Limited

To find out about all our publications,
please visit **www.thamesandhudson.com**.
There you can subscribe to our e-newsletter,
browse or download our current catalogue,
and buy any titles that are in print.

CONTENTS

INTRODUCTION

For us Scandinavians, well-produced, carefully crafted design is just part of everyday life, which we can sometimes take for granted.

OPPOSITE 'Korint' cabinet, 2014, by Snickeriet

OVERLEAF 'Egg' chair, 1958, by Arne Jacobsen, and other designs manufactured by Republic of Fritz Hansen

The history of Nordic design is fascinating, and researching it has been equally absorbing, but discovering so many new talents has been even more rewarding. Most books on the subject begin with looking at the climate of the region. Scandinavia, located in the colder, northern reaches of Europe, has been viewed as a less than welcoming place to work, although celebrated for its mild summers and the stunning spectacle of the aurora lights displays. Living in these volcanic, arctic, rainy, marine and mountainous landscapes has meant that its inhabitants have always had challenges to overcome.

This, of course, led to a tradition of product design that has evolved to focus on usefulness and durability. Nordic designs are almost always geared towards practicality, taking into account the surrounding natural world and its resources. The peoples of Scandinavia come from a mostly agricultural background, and it is readily apparent that a heritage of fishermen and farmers who relied on high-quality tools is still deeply instilled in the Nordic DNA. Well-produced, carefully crafted design is widely available and affordable. When I was a child, even the school chairs were designed by Arne Jacobsen, and today it is noticeable that everything from aeroplane interiors, libraries, offices and even kindergartens possess that element of clever, thoughtful design that has become synonymous with restrained, timeless elegance. But for us Scandinavians, it's just a part of everyday life that we possibly take for granted.

It was in the 1950s that the world really began to take note, and Scandinavian design became a globally recognized and popular design style.

The origins of Nordic design can be traced back to the end of the nineteenth century and the beginnings of the twentieth. Finnish ceramics company Arabia (p. 16) was founded in 1873, and the Exposition Universelle of 1900, in Paris, ushered in a new confidence about the future of Scandinavian design. Some of the well-known figures of the time were Norwegian painter, illustrator and textile designer Gerhard Munthe, who was on the board of the National Gallery of Norway from 1892 to 1905, and architect Herman Gesellius, who designed the Finnish Pavilion for the 1900 Exposition Universelle, along with the Rörstrand porcelain manufacturer, based in Sweden. Social responsibility was already a factor, as seen in an exhibition devoted to designs for the home, held at the Liljevalchs Art Gallery, in Stockholm, in 1917.

It was in the 1950s, however, that the world really began to take note, and Scandinavian design became a globally recognized and popular design style. The term 'Scandinavian', when used in conjunction with design, is misleading, as each of the four countries that together make up the region – Finland, Norway, Sweden and Denmark – have their own histories, traditions and aesthetics. Together with Iceland, they represent the New Nordic Design.

With one-third of the country's landmass located within the Arctic Circle, the people of Finland belong both to the Baltic and Scandinavian ethnic groups. Many of its art and design institutions were formed in the late 1870s, following the success of the Arabia porcelain factory, based in Helsinki. Following the establishment of Finnish independence from Russia in 1917, the Milan Triennale in 1933 marked the wider recognition of the applied arts in Finland. Today, the Finnish design scene is flourishing, with designers such as Joanna Laajisto (p. 142) leading the way in commercial design spaces, or Aalto + Aalto (p. 48), who create objects in collaboration with such established Finnish brands as Iittala.

Norway is among the most northerly regions of Europe, and is sparsely populated, owing to its mountains and dense forests. The country gained independence in 1905, after the dissolution of a union with Sweden that dated back to 1814. The nineteenth-century flowering of national romanticism in architecture and the applied arts was also one of the driving forces behind Norwegian design; before that, practical objects for the home, alongside national costumes, had been passed down through the generations, created and improved during the colder months. Modernism began to gain popularity in the early 1940s, but after the Second World War a crisis of confidence led to the production of work with an inward-looking, cultural distinctiveness, an approach that has perhaps contributed to the country not achieving the same level of success as its neighbours.

The modern use of natural materials represents a new way of thinking for Norway's new design talents, including Lars Beller Fjetland (p. 64), who won the Elle Decoration UK New Designer Award 2013; Everything Elevated (p. 94) and Hunting & Narud (p. 134). Norway, once one of the poorest countries of Europe, has become one of the richest owing to its North Sea revenues, and is currently the world's third-largest exporter of oil, suggesting a returning confidence both to the design scene and to the country as a whole.

The design traditions of Sweden, at least in its modern guise, can be traced to the eighteenth century, when King Gustav III favoured a style inspired by neoclassicism, which was fashionable in Europe, and especially France, and emphasized lightness, comfort, simplicity and a feeling of space. Later, the Biedermeier style, popular in Germany during the early part of the nineteenth century, with its use of blond woods, birch and maple, made its way to Sweden.

The clean and functional designs suited a liberal democracy, celebrating individual freedom that creates solutions for society (Ikea, one of the modern-day giants of Swedish design, has reinforced the point that good design can be affordable). At the 1925 Exposition internationale des arts décoratifs et industriels modernes in Paris, the Swedish Pavilion showcased these two styles, which came together with a delicacy and focus on modernism and simplicity. Today, the great interior design found in Stockholm's high-end hotels, along with the work of newcomers such as Objecthood (p. 180), paves the way for the next generation of design talents.

Denmark, the small, flat country between Germany and Sweden, is possibly one of Scandinavia's most successful countries in terms of design. The furniture school at the Royal Danish Academy of Fine Arts, led by the legendary furniture designer Kaare Klint, played a vital role in the education of and establishing design foundations for future generations. Since the country had few raw materials, Danish designers focused instead on perfecting the craft of long-lasting furniture, making use of local materials. Unlike designers in Sweden, Danes believe that the functional aspect of design has always been present, and instead perfected exciting designs for practical homes, which became extremely popular in the United States and Europe in the 1950s and '60s. Designers behind brands such as Hay (p. 120), Gubi (p. 112) and Normann Copenhagen (p. 168) look to the design traditions of companies such as Carl Hansen & Son and furniture designers including Hans J. Wegner, Finn Juhl (p. 24) or Arne Jacobsen, creating objects that are influenced by the principles of the masters, but modernized for the twenty-first century.

Although not part of Scandinavia, Iceland is very much part of the New Nordic design scene. Sitting just beneath the Arctic Circle, with one of the most active volcanic regions in the world, it

is seen by outsiders as a changeable, challenging
country. Because of its severe weather, objects
have had to be highly functional, and it wasn't
until the late nineteenth century that beauty
and design were encouraged in the industrial
crafts. As the expense of travelling abroad
became prohibitive, making it impossible for
future designers to gain a degree, in 1939 the
School of Applied Arts, in Reykjavik, was
established. A ban on the importing of furniture
in the 1950s and '60s resulted in the opening of
several small-scale factories, which employed such
notable designers as Gunnar Magnússon, who
designed the 'Apollo' chair in 1967, inspired by
NASA's Saturn V moon rocket. Artists such as
Olafur Eliasson (p. 88) have brought attention to the
use of light, creating art installations that transcend
their Scandinavian origins to reach an international
audience. With the coming together of new design
studios and furniture-makers, including Spark

Design Space (p. 198) or Færid (p. 98), Iceland
is now recognized as one of the freshest places
to find new talent.

Today, the countries of Scandinavia are
forming new design alliances by producing
talent from their own design institutions. These
schools attract international students from across
the world, attracted by the enduring appeal of
Scandinavia's design heritage, who in exchange
create new products that have global influences
but are still rooted in the demographic focus
on functionality and long-lasting quality. In
this book, interviews with some of these up-and-
coming talents at the centre of the design world,
along with profiles on some of the old masters
of Scandinavian design, are complemented
by thoughts from the current international
commentators – bloggers, journalists and style
editors – all of whom are devotees of the New
Nordic Design.

PART 1

INFLUENTIAL FIGURES

ARABIA

ABOVE 'Piilopaikka'
series, by Piia Keto

TOP Swedish textile
artist Louise Adelborg

OPPOSITE 'Tuokio' series,
by Helorinne & Kallio

Founded in 1873 by the Swedish company Rörstrand, and now owned by Fiskars, the Finnish ceramics company Arabia has produced kitchenware and tableware with a consumer-orientated aesthetic ever since. In the nineteenth century, when the company was founded, ceramics production in Finland was still in its infancy, but a booming economy ensured that demand, and the company, grew quickly. The original factory was located in the Toukola district of Helsinki (the building now houses the Aalto University School of Arts, Design and Architecture).

By 1875, Arabia already employed 110 people, and in 1900 the company received a gold medal at the Exposition Universelle in Paris. Many well-known ceramics artists and designers have been associated with Arabia over the years, including Ulla Procopé (whose designs include the 'Liekki' and 'Valencia' series, from 1958 and 1960), Esteri Tomula (who worked at the company from 1947–84, producing the 'Fennica' and 'Krokus' series), Birger Kaipiainen ('Paratiisi' series, 1969) and Kaj Franck, who was appointed artistic director of the company in 1945; he also designed the 'Kilta' range in 1953, which was relaunched under the name 'Teema' in 1981.

Arabia's successes continued into the new millennium, and the company continues to work with talented designers. When Helsinki was named World Design Capital for 2012, Arabia marked the occasion by producing a new mug design, the 'Kotikaupunki' series. The company has also embraced popular culture by producing mugs and tableware decorated with Moomin characters, from the well-loved children's books by Tove Jansson, and Angry Birds.

DYSTHE DESIGN

The man behind Dysthe Design, Norwegian furniture designer Sven Ivar Dysthe, left his mark on furniture history by inventing a new laminating technique. Born in Oslo in 1931, Dysthe had originally trained as a carpenter, before attending the Royal College of Art, London. While a student there, he created the college's gift casket for Queen Elizabeth II's coronation in 1953. A year later, he went to work for architect Orla Mølgaard-Nielsen in Copenhagen, and quickly became inspired by the Scandinavian design movement.

The simplicity and functionality that is the hallmark of Scandinavian furniture became the basis for Dysthe's own approach to design, and in 1958 he established his own design studio. He won a furniture competition in Norway with an armchair that used a new lamination technique, which caught the eye of the major furniture companies. His breakthrough came in 1960, when Norwegian firm Dokka Bondemøbler presented Dysthe's '1001' armchair at the IMM Cologne furniture fair, where his bold design of steel, rosewood and black leather was an instant success. During the rest of the decade, other iconic designs soon followed, including the 'Laminette' chair and the 'Planet' series.

Dysthe famously observed: 'When aesthetics, function and form merge and become one whole and you think, aha, of course!, then you have succeeded. Good food will melt on your tongue. Good design should melt within yourself. So simple, and yet so challenging.'

OPPOSITE 'Planet' chair, 1965

BELOW 'Laminette' armchair, 1964, relaunched by Rybo

ARTEK

ABOVE 'Tea Trolley 901', 1937,
by Alvar Aalto for Artek

TOP 'Armchair 401', 1933,
by Alvar Aalto for Artek,
reinterpreted by Hella Jongerius

OPPOSITE 'Tea Trolley 900',
1936, by Alvar Aalto for Artek

OVERLEAF Artek home
interiors, 2011 (left); 'Tea Trolley
901' and 'Armchair 401' (right)

Finnish furniture company Artek was founded in 1935 by designers Alvar Aalto and his wife Aino Aalto, arts promoter Maire Gullichsen and art historian Nils-Gustav Hahl, with an emphasis on quality in terms of technique, production methods and materials. Today it is based in Helsinki, where the firm also operates four retail spaces – a flagship store in the Esplanadi, Artek 2nd Cycle, Artek Aitta and the Vitra Loves Artek – and has offices in New York, Tokyo, Stockholm and Berlin. The company is now owned by Vitra.

Among the earliest designs produced by Artek were Alvar and Aino Aalto's furniture and lamps for the Paimio Sanatorium (1929–33), including the 'Paimio' chair, designed specifically for tuberculosis patients who had to endure long periods of sitting. The chair, now considered an iconic piece of Finnish design, is in the permanent collection of the Museum of Modern Art, New York. Another early design, 'Stool E60', is used by Apple in their stores, while their glass designs are now produced by Iittala.

Artek produces furniture, lighting and accessories by Scandinavian masters Tapio Wirkkala, Eero Aarnio, Jørn Utzon, Juha Leiviskä, and many others, as well as collaborating with architects, designers and artists from around the world, including Hella Jongerius, Konstantin Grcic, and Shigeru Ban, who designed Artek's exhibition pavilion for the Milan Triennale 2007; the pavilion was later installed, temporarily, outside the Design Museum, Helsinki.

FINN JUHL

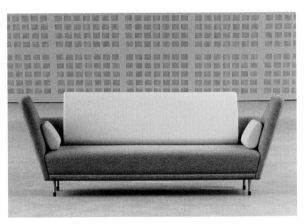

ABOVE 'Egyptian' dining chair, 1949;
'109' dining chair, 1946; '57' sofa, 1957

One of the leading architects and designers of the mid-twentieth century is the great Finn Juhl. He was the designer behind the introduction of Danish Modern to the US in the 1950s and '60s, and remains a revered name in product and interior design in Scandinavia today. Although Juhl wanted to be an art historian, his father, a textile wholesaler, persuaded him to study architecture instead. Juhl attended the Royal Danish Academy of Fine Arts in 1930–4, where he studied under Kay Fisker, an architect associated with the Danish Functionalism movement. Following his studies, Juhl worked for the next ten years for architectural firm Vilhelm Lauritzen. While there, he designed the interior for the Radio Building, for which he received the C. F. Hansen prize for young architects in 1943.

Two years later, Juhl left the company and set up on his own, and began to focus on furniture. He had previously shown furniture designs at the Cabinetmakers' Guild Exhibitions, an important showcase for his designs in that they emphasized craftsmanship over mass-production. His first efforts, including the 'Pelican' chair, designed in 1939 and first produced in 1940, were not well received. It was not until 1948, when his work was noticed by the American architect, Edgar Kaufmann, Jr., that his fortunes began to change. Kaufmann featured Juhl's designs in a lengthy article in *Interiors* magazine, and in 1951 his work was shown at the 'Good Design' exhibition, in Chicago. During the 1950s, Juhl won five gold medals at the Milan Triennale, representing a high point in his career.

Over the following decades his designs diminished in popularity. In 2010, however, one of his sofa designs was reissued by Danish furniture company OneCollection and won a Wallpaper Design Award. Although Juhl's legacy is in his designs for furniture, he was also an interior designer of some note, and designed the interiors for the Bing & Grøndahl in Copenhagen (1946) and the Trusteeship Council Chamber for the UN Building in New York (1951–2). Today, Finn Juhl's house next to the Ordrupgaard Museum, where he lived until his death in 1989, is a must-visit destination.

'One cannot create happiness with beautiful objects, but one can spoil quite a lot of happiness with bad ones.'

BELOW Sideboard, 1955, for Bovirke

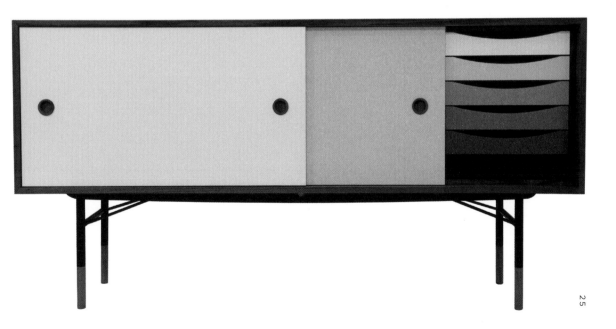

OPPOSITE 'Sofa 968', 1930s, by Josef Frank; 'Stool 647', 1936

BELOW 'Arm Chair 3543 Oxford'

Interior-design company Svenskt Tenn was founded in 1924, in Stockholm, by Estrid Ericson, who began by offering affordable pewter ware designed by artist Nils Fougstedt, produced in the workshop behind the shop. The following year, the company received a gold medal at the Paris Expo.

In 1927, the firm moved to its present location, and soon began to enter into a series of fruitful collaborations, including partnerships with Swedish architects Uno Åhrén and Björn Trägårdh, and, most notably, designer Josef Frank, an Austrian émigré who joined Svenskt Tenn in 1934 and worked with Ericson until his death in 1967. In 1975, the company was sold; four years later Ann Wall took over as managing director and became instrumental in transforming it into a profitable business for the modern age. In honour of her achievements, the Ann Wall Design Prize is awarded annually to celebrate new design talent.

The company is steadfast in its commitment to Swedish craftsmanship, and its output, with very few exceptions, is made in Sweden. Most of the furniture has been produced at the same workshops since the 1950s. Frank's legacy also continues: after his death, he left behind some two thousand furniture sketches and 160 textile designs, of which about forty are still in production. But although Frank's designs remain the core of the company's product range, Svenskt Tenn is also embracing the world of modern design, and has hosted exhibitions, including 'Patterns of the Biosphere', in which four artists translated research from the Beijer Institute, Royal Swedish Academy of Sciences, into a series of posters, and 'Three Decades', which re-imagined set designs from films of the 1930s, '50s and '80s with furniture from Svenskt Tenn.

KÄLLEMO

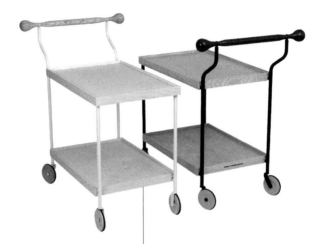

ABOVE 'Darjeeling' trollies, by Anna Kraitz

OPPOSITE, ABOVE 'Caravaggio' recliners, by Johan Linton

OPPOSITE, BELOW 'Concave' chaise longue, by Jonas Bohlin

Furniture company Källemo was founded after the Second World War as a carpenters' cooperative, producing mostly bentwood furniture. In the 1960s the company was taken over by Sven Lundh, who took the company in a new direction. After the war there had been a shortage in housing in Sweden, and the 'million programme' was launched, in which one million new flats were to be built. The flats all had to be furnished, leading to an all-time peak of production in the furniture business.

Lundh explains: 'At the time, quality was measured in technical terms (strength of glued joints, for example). But good quality is judged by the eye, not by the back. If a piece of furniture is used day and night for two years without showing any signs of wear, but you cannot bear the sight of it anymore, then it is bad quality. You can always repair a bent leg, but not a bad form. So good

quality has to stand up to being looked at, year after year. Good quality is visual quality.'

That definition of quality was the opposite of the established view, which dictated that technical function and testing methods were paramount. In 1980, at a furniture fair in Stockholm, Lundh saw a piece that defined his view of quality: a chair designed by Jonas Bohlin, in raw steel and concrete, as his graduation project. The 'Concrete' chair went on to have a huge impact on Swedish design. It was only produced in one hundred copies and commands high prices at auction. Today, the company collaborates with such legendary furniture designers as Sigurdur Gustafsson (p. 40); Mats Theselius, a leading designer and artist in Sweden; and Komplot Design, the firm behind the 'Non' rubber chair. Källemo retains their goal of continually presenting something new, whether in design, function or material.

REPUBLIC OF FRITZ HANSEN

The long history of the company stretches back to 1872, when furniture-maker Fritz Hansen, originally from Nakskov, in southern Denmark, obtained a trade licence. By 1887, Hansen, now in partnership with his son Christian, set up their workshop in central Copenhagen. Christian Hansen soon realized that to make the design and production process simpler and more cost-effective, new methods had to be explored. He used steam to bend the wood into new shapes, a process that was revolutionary at the time, but by the 1930s had become the company's signature.

In 1934, the company began a collaboration with the relatively unknown designer Arne Jacobsen, who had won a silver medal at the Paris Art Deco Fair in 1925, while still a student, for his chair design. The partnership lasted until into the 1950s (with a brief hiatus in 1943, when Jacobsen fled Denmark during the war). Among his designs for Fritz Hansen were such iconic chairs as 'Egg' and 'Swan' (both 1958), as well as the 'Ant' (1952), 'Series 7' (1955) and 'Grand Prix' (1957) designs.

Another key collaboration was with Hans J. Wegner, whose 'China' chair has been produced by the company since 1944. Wegner designed more than five hundred chairs, including the 'Peacock', 'J16' rocking chair and 'The Chair', of which one hundred are still mass-produced; the rest are collector's items. Poul Kjærholm, Sidse Werner, Piet Hein and Børge Mogensen are among the other designers who formed lasting partnerships with the company. Today, the Republic of Fritz Hansen works with a new generation of designers, including Cecilie Manz (p. 150).

ABOVE 'Series 7' chair, by Arne Jacobsen, and 'Essay' table, by Cecilie Manz

OPPOSITE 'Egg' chair, by Arne Jacobsen

OVERLEAF 'Ant', 'Grand Prix', 'Lily' and 'Series 7' chair designs

TORBJØRN AFDAL

Norwegian furniture designer Torbjørn Afdal was one of the groundbreaking designers of the twentieth century, and is still revered as one of the country's most productive in the postwar period.

After graduating from the National Academy of the Arts, in Oslo, in 1946, Afdal started work at the design studio Bruksbo, where he became one of its leading designers – and later in Scandinavia. In Norway he is well known as the designer of the office of Gro Harlem Brundtland, the country's first female prime minister, as well as the parliamentarians' chairs and tables, and his designs have been famously purchased by First Lady Jacqueline Kennedy for the White House.

In 1958, Afdal took part in the Deutsche Handwerksmesse in Munich, and two years later participated in the Milan Triennale to much acclaim. During the 1960s, Afdal's work took a more architectonic direction, and he began to use teak and rosewood in combination with leather and steel. The 'Broadway' and 'Hunter' chairs are among his iconic designs, and today his furniture commands high prices at auction.

Torbjørn Afdal died in 1999, but his legacy lives on. In 2013 the exhibition 'Norwegian Icons', held in Oslo, Tokyo and New York, included several of his furniture designs.

OPPOSITE, ABOVE 'Krobo' bench, 1960, produced by Bruksbo

OPPOSITE, BELOW Stereo cabinet, *c.* 1970, produced by Bruksbo

BELOW 'Elton' chair, *c.* 1960, produced by Nesjestranda Furnituredolectio

SWEDESE

ABOVE 'Happy' armchair

TOP 'Manga' chairs and 'Breeze' table,
by Monica Förster

OPPOSITE 'Happy' easy chair
and 'Breeze' side table

OVERLEAF 'Spin' stools by Staffan Holm,
with 'Stella' chairs and 'Bespoke' table

Swedish furniture-maker Swedese has produced timeless designs since the very beginnings of Scandinavian design's golden age. The company was founded in 1945 by brothers Yngve and Jerker Ekström, along with Sven Bertil Sjöqvist, and flourished under Yngve Ekström's leadership until his death over forty years later.

Along with Alvar Aalto, Arne Jacobsen and Poul Kjærholm, Yngve Ekström was at the centre of a generation of designers who contributed to the international fame of Scandinavian design. In addition to his day-to-day duties running the company, he designed the furniture, headquarters building, logo and catalogues, and even the company Christmas cards. Ekström's best-known design is the 'Lamino' armchair, from 1956, which is still in production today. In 1999, the 'Lamino' was voted by *Sköna Hem* magazine as the best Swedish furniture design of the twentieth century.

Today the company has a showroom in Stockholm, but its headquarters and main factory are in Vaggeryd, in Småland, the traditional heartland of Swedish furniture production. A second factory is in Äng, outside Nässjö. Among its roster of current designers are Mats Broberg and Johan Ridderstråle, who designed the 'Kite' series; design studio Claesson Koivisto Rune, with the 'Caravelle' chair and 'Continental' seating system among their designs; Monica Förster, who designed the 'Breeze' series of tables; and Staffan Holm, the designer behind the 'Spin' series of stacking stools.

'Swedese's ideals are the same today as they have been for the past sixty years. We want to create beautiful furniture for the future.'

SIGURDUR GUSTAFSSON

Furniture and industrial designer Sigurdur Gustafsson was born on Christmas Eve in Akureyri, a town in northern Iceland, in 1962. His father was a carpenter, and this early exposure to form and materials proved to be a seminal influence in his later choice of career.

After graduating from Oslo School of Architecture and Design in 1990, Gustafsson joined the office of Cullberg Architects in Gothenburg, Sweden, before setting up own practice in 1995. Two years later, he embarked on a fruitful collaboration with Swedish furniture brand Källemo (p. 28), for whom he has created many now-classic designs, including the 'Skyscraper' shelving unit, 'Skyseat' chair, 'Koncept' table and the 'DNA' steel magazine rack.

Gustafsson believes that the process of making furniture without the use of screws or glue is a good exercise in exploring the integrity of an object. He focuses on the idea that design is more than just working with forms, and that good design lies in how material and form unite. In the short space of Iceland's design history, Sigurdur Gustafsson has emerged as a leading figure in a new generation of creators of iconic contemporary furniture.

THESE PAGES 'Tango' chair, 1998, produced by Källemo

'I focus on the idea; design is more than just working with forms. You must learn to see and explore.'

PART 2

THE DESIGNERS

&TRADITION

Danish company &tradition produces classic designs by designers such as Verner Panton and Arne Jacobsen, while providing a platform for new designers, including Sofie Refer and All The Way To Paris. They combine craftsmanship with modern design, following the Nordic tradition of high quality.

WHAT IS THE BACKGROUND OF YOUR COMPANY?

We are a Danish design firm, set up in 2010 with the principle of tradition tied to innovation. Our library of furniture and lighting designs spans the 1930s to the present day, and includes works by internationally renowned designers.

WHAT INSPIRES YOU WHEN YOU ARE CREATING NEW COLLECTIONS?

We connect with the old masters, while giving space to new names to design future classics. We see a kinship between the designers of the last century, who were avant-garde in their time, and the designers of today, who are creating the groundbreaking icons of tomorrow.

WHO ARE THE MAIN DESIGNERS AND PRODUCERS YOU WORK WITH TODAY?

We collaborate with a range of designers, including All The Way To Paris, Benjamin Hubert, Jaime Hayon, Lex Pott, Luca Nichetto, Mia Hamborg, Norm Architects (p. 172), Ontwerpduo, Sami Kallio, Samuel Wilkinson, Sofie Refer, Space Copenhagen (p. 194) and Victor Vetterlein.

OPPOSITE 'Copenhagen' pendant light, by Space Copenhagen; 'Catch' chair by Jaime Hayon and 'NA2' table by Norm Architects

BELOW 'FlowerPot' lamp, 1969, by Verner Panton

HOW DOES DANISH DESIGN DIFFER FROM THAT OF OTHER COUNTRIES, BOTH SCANDINAVIAN AND WORLDWIDE?

Danish design is great when it comes to functionality and high-quality materials designed in a modern way. We are proud to represent some of the best classic designs, and to collaborate with some of the best designers working today – something we have achieved in a very short time.

WHAT DOES NORDIC DESIGN REPRESENT TO YOU TODAY?

Craft meets art. Function meets form. Material meets potential. This is our Nordic tradition and heritage. We aim to bring these values to contemporary design – reshaping, redefining and reinventing materials, techniques and forms. We respect nature, which provides our raw materials, and we believe in design that is made to last.

THESE PAGES 'Utzon' lamp, designed by Jørn Utzon; 'Fly' sofa, by Space Copenhagen; and 'Hoof' table by Samuel Wilkinson

AALTO + AALTO

Having established their design studio in 2010, in Helsinki, Elina and Klaus Aalto share a desire to create functional and emotional objects inspired by their surroundings. They have produced designs for Kekkilä, Selki-asema and SAVEtheC, and taken part in the 'Hirameki Design × Finland' exhibition at the Living Design Center, Tokyo.

WHAT HAS BEEN THE MOST SIGNIFICANT PRODUCT FOR YOUR COMPANY?

We started working together when we had already been a couple for ten years. It started with a joint project: a bunk bed for our children. As designers, we couldn't help but approach the task as if it were a real product, and not just something for our home. The 'Maja' bunk bed ended up being shown in several exhibitions, and we are currently working on a new version. The project was a good test in that it showed us we could work well together, and both bring something to the table. With our projects, it's impossible to say in the end who contributed what. They are a good mix of us both.

DO YOU FIND INSPIRATION IN YOUR SURROUNDINGS IN HELSINKI?

We have both been inspired by the Seurasaari Open-Air Museum, which has a collection of old houses from around Finland. We had visited on school trips as children, but now perhaps we are old enough to appreciate the different building techniques, the logic behind them and the skill with which they were made. Although we are curious about new things, we also appreciate the past.

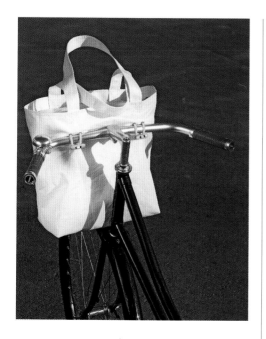

ABOVE 'NonBicycleBag', produced by SAVEtheC

OPPOSITE 'Take Out' cabinet, next to a classic chair design by Alvar Aalto

WHAT DO YOU BELIEVE IS SIGNIFICANT FOR DESIGN TODAY?

A design today starts as it always has: with a problem or challenge that needs to be solved. Conditions change, so the problems change and the answers must change, too. If we look at now compared with ten years ago, ecology has become a built-in part of the process.

WHAT DO YOU STRIVE FOR IN REGARDS TO FINNISH DESIGN?

Finnish design is very democratic: it is genuinely part of everyday life. Finland was a poor, rural society a hundred years ago, and has changed very rapidly. But our past shows us that our designs are simple and practical. The concept of luxury is quite foreign to us. We aim to make things that are not seasonal or fashionable, but that live on for decades.

WHICH OF YOUR PRODUCTS DO YOU CONSIDER TO BE YOUR STAND-OUT ITEMS?

The 'Vakka' box for Iittala feels like a big achievement, because of all of our designs, it is the one that has the most users. Much of our work only exists as prototypes – and we feel that they are valuable – but design is meant to be used by people.

With 'Vakka', it's exciting to know that there are people all over the world who have the product in their homes.

WHAT DOES NORDIC DESIGN TODAY REPRESENT TO YOU?

Nordic design is living some kind of renaissance with new companies like Muuto (p. 156) and Hay (p. 120) becoming very established quite quickly, and old companies like Iittala and Lundia reinventing themselves. It is also without boundaries, with companies working together with designers from around the area. Strictly Finnish design is quite hard to define now that company ownership might be in another country, and the designers might come from another country. Still, Artek (p. 20), for example, is considered Finnish because of its roots and history.

ARE THERE ANY FAVOURITE PLACES IN SCANDINAVIA THAT YOU ARE INSPIRED BY?

Our whole family is in love with Iceland. The scenery is amazing, like from another world. The people are very approachable and warm, and Reykjavik is a strange but wonderful combination of rough and cute.

CAMILLA AKERSVEEN

As part of the '100% Norway' exhibition for the 2014 London Design Festival, up-and-coming designer Camilla Akersveen created the 'Mindful Eating' series to enhance our sensory experience of food. She produces her own prototypes to better understand how the design will communicate with the materials.

WHEN DID YOU DISCOVER THAT DESIGN WAS YOUR CALLING?

My interest in design started during a one-year university preparation at the Design Institute in Oslo, which opened my eyes to interiors and furniture design. It was through a special project, for which I designed a stool, that I suddenly got a special feeling for furniture design. In 2014, I graduated with an MA in interior and furniture design from the Oslo National Academy of the Arts. As a designer, I aspire to create products that are playful and aesthetic, while also being multifunctional and useful in daily life.

WHERE DO YOU GO IN OSLO FOR INSPIRATION?

I often find inspiration while riding the tram in Oslo. I daydream while looking at the people around me and the urban landscape, which is constantly changing.

DO THE YOUNGER GENERATION OF NORWEGIAN DESIGNERS FACE CHALLENGES?

We have had only a few famous designers throughout our history, and we are not a country known for its design, as Denmark is. But I think the younger generation of designers in Norway is eager to show their talent. And that maybe separates us from other countries.

HOW DO YOU DESIGN AN OBJECT?

If I already have an idea of what to make – tableware, for example – I start by looking back at history to see how the object has evolved over time and how different cultures use tableware. After building my knowledge, I start a drawing process. Later on, I take my sketches and draw them in a 3D program. I choose the shape I like best and make a model of it, and then try the product on different user groups. The final form is decided after going through several different trials. At the end of that process, I can make it in the right material.

WHAT DOES THE FUTURE HOLD FOR NORWEGIAN DESIGN?

I think Norwegian design can only go upwards. More and more people pay attention to us. Norwegian design has a unique quality and distinctiveness. There are many talented designers in Norway. And it's hard to just name a few names. So I think it's better to say that I get inspired by the young design community in Norway.

JOHN ASTBURY

After studying anthropology and sociology as an undergraduate, John Astbury received an MFA in industrial design from the University College of Arts, Crafts and Design, Sweden, in 2011. Since then, he has exhibited in New York, London, Tokyo, Paris and Stockholm, and received international acclaim after winning the 2010 Muuto Talent Award and an Elle Interior Award in 2012.

TELL ME ABOUT YOUR HISTORY AS A DESIGNER

I began my studies in England, and then moved to Sweden to gain an education in design, where I completed an MFA in industrial design in 2011. My work has been shown in Europe, Scandinavia and the US, and has won a Muuto Talent Award 2010, an Elle Decoration Award 2012 and a Bo Bedre Design Award 2013. During my studies, I worked alongside Bengt Brummer and Karin Wallenbeck under the collective name WhatsWhat. In 2011 we released the 'Greta' pendant lamp with Svenskt Tenn (p. 26), followed by the 'Pull' lamp for Muuto (p. 156) in 2012. Since establishing my own studio in 2013, I have continued to work in several collaborations.

WHAT ARE YOUR KEY INSPIRATIONS?

My method is based on words. It is conversations: overheard and misheard, whispers and lies. These are my starting points. It may be a passing comment, or a long discussion, but words always form a key component to my work – taking these words or dialogues and turning them into a visual or tactile form.

ABOVE 'Greta' lamp, 2011, produced by Svenskt Tenn

OPPOSITE 'Fade' collection, designed with Kyuhyung Cho

WHO ARE THE MAIN DESIGNERS YOU WORK WITH TODAY?

I currently work with Swedish firm TAF, Kyuhyung Cho and Karin Wallenbeck, but this is always shifting. As long as I can work with interesting people and on interesting projects, I am happy.

HOW DOES SWEDISH DESIGN DIFFER FROM THAT OF OTHER COUNTRIES?

It is such a hard question to answer. It means very different things to different people. I think the surrounding environment is hugely influential on any group or designer. It is a cliché, but even at its most urban, the water and the forest are never far away in Sweden. It is a common heritage.

DO YOU HAVE ANY FAVOURITE PLACES IN SCANDINAVIA THAT INSPIRE YOU?

I love Stockholm and the archipelago. But inspiration really comes from the people I am with. So I would say bars and cafés are the places for me. Perhaps brunch at Babylon in Stockholm would be a good start to a Saturday.

WHAT DOES NORDIC DESIGN TODAY REPRESENT TO YOU?

Aesthetically, material and craft are prevalent. There is often talk about honesty and efficiency, the simplicity of purpose, and I think that is still true, but it is also about questioning these values and creating new perspectives of design in a wider context. To me, it is the meeting point between these two positions. It's a good place to be.

BARE MØBLER

Bare Møbler began in 2003, as a Bergen Academy exhibition project. The company's name, which translates as 'only furniture', is a collaboration between furniture designers Karl Marius Sveen and his partner Ørjan Djønne. Based in Bergen and Oslo, the duo's products exemplify Norwegian design values such as simplicity, understatement, humour and the natural world.

HOW IS DESIGNING IN NORWAY DIFFERENT FROM OTHER COUNTRIES?

Because of the Internet, social media and cheap plane tickets, it's not that different anymore. We might benefit from being a smaller country in the sense that almost everyone knows everybody else who is doing some kind of creative work. There is also an awareness about design by the government now, which makes it easier to get financial support for projects that promote Norwegian design abroad.

BELOW 'Twisted Star' table, by Karl Marius Sveen and Ørjan Djønne, manufactured by RBM Furniture

OPPOSITE 'Wings' chair, prototype, by Karl Marius Sveen

WHAT IS YOUR BACKGROUND?

There are two of us in the company. I was born and raised in Oslo, but studied at the Bergen Academy of Art and Design in Norway. I draw inspiration from the Scandinavian way of thinking and living. For me, furniture should be easy and simple, with both aesthetic and functional values. Ørjan was born in Odda, a small village in the west of Norway. We studied together at Bergen, and have always loved carpentry, woodworking and making things. Ørjan has worked as an interior architect and furniture designer for ten years now. Our projects cover everything from public buildings and concert halls to bars and restaurants.

WHAT INSPIRES YOUR WORK?

People who are not afraid of following their dreams while thinking outside the box. I can be inspired by autumn leaves or a hot Miami night, or maybe some old wooden tool. Working through projects thoroughly and investigating new production methods with old techniques also inspires me. For Ørjan, it's furniture-makers like John Maloof and George Nakashima; for me, interior designers such as David Collins and Roman and Williams are inspirational, as is Therme Vals by Peter Zumthor. Meeting fellow designers is also an interesting learning process.

DO YOU HAVE ANY FAVOURITE PLACES IN NORWAY OR SCANDINAVIA?

The tomb of Emanuel Vigeland, the Norwegian painter and brother of Gustav Vigeland, who created the famous sculptures in Frogner Park, one of Oslo's best-kept art secrets. The Norwegian Museum of Cultural History at Bygdøy is an outdoor museum showcasing Norway's building history. We think Copenhagen is a wonderful, inspiring place for a designer: a trip to Klampenborg, a suburb of the city, is highly recommended.

ARE YOU INFLUENCED BY ANY PARTICULAR DESIGNER?

We are hugely inspired by the Danish designer Hans J. Wegner, as well as Sven Ivar Dysthe of Dysthe Design (p. 18). Our future will hopefully include more multidisciplinary projects, linking furniture, fashion, even jewelry. We should all be collaborating towards a common goal.

ABOVE 'Good News' table, by Karl Marius Sveen, manufactured by Mokasser

OPPOSITE 'EasyFlex' chair, prototype, by Karl Marius Sveen

BELLER

Lars Beller Fjetland credits growing up on the west coast of Norway with instilling an early fascination with the natural world and its materials, along with a recognition of the importance of function. Today, he designs interiors, furniture and lighting, and has won such prestigious awards as Elle Decoration UK's New Designer 2013 and Young Designer of the Year 2012, as well as Norwegian Designer of the Year 2014.

ARE THERE ANY ADVANTAGES TO BEING A DESIGNER IN NORWAY?

I'm not sure if designing in Norway is significantly different to working in any other place in the world. As designers we all deal with the same challenges, and we use a lot of the same tools to solve them. There are some advantages to living in a smaller city like Bergen. Here, there is far less visual noise, which tends to clutter my mind. I also enjoy the feeling of being part of a community, surrounded by friends and familiar faces. I honestly find it hard to get inspired in a large metropolis, as I never seem to find the time to really dig deep into anything. I find myself gradually turning into a more superficial individual, resulting in a loss of both curiosity and creativity. I guess my mind isn't really made to cope with the frantic pace of a busy city, and I think this is something that a lot of Norwegians can relate to. If you delve far enough, you might find something real, innovative and beautiful. That is why I chose to do this for a living.

ABOVE 'Pomme' paperweight, produced by Hem

OPPOSITE 'Drifted' stool, 2012, produced by Discipline

WHAT IS YOUR BACKGROUND?

I graduated from the Bergen Academy of Art and Design in 2012, a year after establishing my own studio. I created my first pieces during my second year there. The 'Re-turned' birds, 'Link' textiles and the 'Drifted' series were all results of playing with materials to understand how and why things work. Both the 'Re-turned' birds and the 'Drifted' series are now produced by the Italian design company Discipline.

WHAT DRIVES YOU MOST IN YOUR WORK?

Nature will always play an important part in my projects. The natural world has found solutions for all of its challenges, and they are all perfect, down to the smallest detail. This drives me to work even harder towards finding the optimal solution to my own challenges.

DO YOU HAVE ANY FAVOURITE PLACES IN NORWAY OR SCANDINAVIA?

I head to the seven mountains around Bergen when I need a time out. A walk through this stunning countryside usually leaves me with a serenity and peace unmatched by anything else.

HOW DO YOU BEGIN THE DESIGN PROCESS?

Each design is unique in its own way, but the set of tools to achieve it are often the same. This is what ties the different projects together, giving them your own particular touch as a designer.

I tend to begin my design processes by studying a specific material, or combination of materials. I investigate the properties and inherent qualities, and let my findings dictate the direction of the project. So far I've been exploring the world of natural materials, a decision that has helped me in finding my path, style and logic. I guess 'driven by curiosity, guided by nature' sums up the way I think, work and live.

ARE THERE ANY DESIGNERS WHOSE WORK YOU PARTICULARLY ADMIRE?

Basically, anything and everything inspires me; it wouldn't really make sense to name any one designer in particular. Idolizing others can interfere with your own development. However, I really enjoy the work of Alvar Aalto (see Artek; p. 20), Ilmari Tapiovaara and Timo Sarpaneva.

I also have a newfound appreciation for the designs of Axel Einar Hjorth and Edvin Helseth.

WHAT ARE THE PROBLEMS FACING NORWEGIAN DESIGN, AS WELL AS OPPORTUNITIES FOR THE FUTURE?

Norwegian design has never been able to match the status of our neighbouring countries, but change is on the horizon. The current design community in Norway is relatively small, but it's buzzing with activity. Young designers are coming together, sharing experiences, ideas and dreams. Most of us see each other as colleagues, rather than competitors. I am convinced that this is the reason behind the success the Norwegian design scene is currently experiencing, as it allows designers to work much more efficiently. It keeps us sharp and inspired, believing that anything is possible.

THESE PAGES 'Touchwood', 2014, produced by Discipline

BERNS HOTEL

The grand old Berns Hotel is a favourite among the design-conscious travelling to Stockholm to experience Swedish design up close. Manager Yvonne Sörensen brings an eye for detail from her five years as CEO of Svenskt Tenn (p. 26).

WHAT IS THE BACKGROUND OF THE DESIGN?

We tried to create a homely atmosphere in our hotel rooms. To do this, we mixed old and new and used international design, including some Swedish designers. When you create a hotel, you also need to think about wear and tear, so the pieces must last better and longer than they would in the home.

WHAT WERE THE KEY INSPIRATIONS BEHIND THE HOTEL?

Before joining Berns Hotel in 2007, I was the CEO of Svenskt Tenn. The interior-design philosophy there has been a great source of inspiration. We tried to choose furniture that lasts, but that also creates a relaxing mix of design and comfort in the rooms. Different colours, shades and styles are mixed together, along with vintage pieces.

HOW DOES SWEDISH DESIGN DIFFER FROM THAT OF OTHER COUNTRIES?

Swedish design, in general, is cleaner, without ornaments, and is geared towards 'practical thinking', using beautiful, sustainable materials that we have available here, such as wood and leather.

ABOVE The 'Robert Berns' suite
OPPOSITE The lobby
OVERLEAF The dining room

BIRGER1962

After twenty-five years in the
fashion industry, Malene Birger
decided to sell her fashion
company By Malene Birger
and move on. Her new venture,
Birger1962, has already taken
part in Maison & Object, Paris,
and been featured in Elle
Decoration UK.

TELL ME ABOUT YOUR NEW COMPANY. WHY DID YOU DECIDE TO SET IT UP?

Birger1962 is a newly established, project-driven design studio. Having worked for more than twenty-five years in fashion, I felt I needed to establish my style in a new field. I like to create complete concepts and universes, where I can offer my own designs in furniture and other objects. Our goal is to collaborate with other creative branches and build bridges between them. With my background, I was craving the opportunity to express myself in a new way.

DO YOU WORK WITH OTHER DESIGNERS?

I don't have any main producers or designers yet. Since the launch of the company in 2014, my team and I are still the driving force. I hope to work with creative teams and colleagues around the world in the future, on different projects. Our main production is in Europe.

WHY DID YOU DECIDE TO MAKE THE MOVE FROM FASHION TO INTERIORS?

I have one life, and for many years I wanted to work in art and interiors. The fashion business had become tougher and tougher; there are no breaks, no rest for inspiration. I felt like a factory and I had enough. Five years ago I decided to change

ABOVE The Copenhagen showroom

OPPOSITE Malene Birger's office in London

direction, sold my shares in By Malene Birger and began setting up Birger1962. I do love fashion, but for now I prefer to buy clothes, rather than design them. But you never know, perhaps I will design clothes again one day.

HOW DO YOU EXPERIENCE DANISH DESIGN IN RELATION TO THAT OF OTHER COUNTRIES, NORDIC AND WORLDWIDE?

It's difficult for me to answer. I was born in Copenhagen, but my style has never been Nordic – not in fashion, and not now. My style is eclectic and 'maximalist', not typically Nordic. I'm more into Arabian culture and ethnic influences. But I do like clean lines, white walls and a lot of light, and that is very Scandinavian. I'm very much into vintage furniture and lamps from the 1970s, which I buy mostly in the US. The Danish design heritage of the 1950s and '60s might differ from that of Sweden and Norway, in that they still have some of the most iconic furniture designs in the world. Classics forever and ever, like Finn Juhl (p. 24), Børge Mogensen, Hans J. Wegner, Arne Jacobsen – the list goes on. Travelling and all the interesting people I meet on my journeys inspire me. Art, films and flea markets are all great sources of inspiration.

WHAT DOES NORDIC DESIGN TODAY REPRESENT TO YOU?

Nordic design is a very strong trend at the moment, and it's everywhere. Food and design are especially influenced by it. It represents clean lines, form, function, soft and natural colours. It's organic, minimalist and focuses on the environment. To me, the Nordic style appears lacking in personality, and everything looks very much the same. But that's my personal opinion. I like to combine different looks, eras and styles.

YOU USE A LOT OF BROWN AND BLACK IN YOUR DESIGNS. WHY?

I don't really know. These colours make me calm, and since I'm very 'noisy' in my styling, I can calm areas down with neutral colours. The brown started to grow on me when I lived in Spain – a great influence from the Moors. But I have begun to develop a feel for colours again. I haven't had that feeling for more than twenty years. It might be because I'm not working with colour cards every day, as I did when I worked in fashion.

WHAT HAS BEEN YOUR GREATEST ACHIEVEMENT SO FAR?

I achieved so much with my two fashion brands, and I came very far with By Malene Birger – I could not ask for more. But if I can enter a completely new business, with no name, fifty-two years old and manage to get a few interesting hotel projects and work with talented people, and still have time for my art, then that must be the greatest achievement of them all. I still have so many ideas, and things I want to do. I did manage to get married before I turned fifty, and that was another happy achievement.

EMILIA BORGTHORSDÓTTIR

Icelandic designer Emilia Borgthorsdóttir is best known for her 'Sebastopol' tables, which were introduced by Coalesse at NeoCon 2011 and won gold. Her work has also been shown at the Salone del Mobile, in Milan, and she has acted as an advocate at DesignMarch.

IS THE NATURAL WORLD AN IMPORTANT INFLUENCE IN YOUR WORK, AS IT IS FOR SO MANY ICELANDIC DESIGNERS?

The three key elements that have the biggest impact on my design are nature, community and Icelandic culture. I grew up in Vestmannaeyjar, off the south coast of Iceland. Surrounded by mountains, volcanos, the ocean and a strong wind blowing in your face, you become very aware of your surroundings. You need to wrestle with it every day, and you have to respect it. The freedom children in Iceland enjoy has also been a big factor, as it allows you to dream and try different things. But there are also drawbacks to growing up in a small, isolated community – you had to be resourceful. Icelandic culture has had a great impact on both my personality and my goals. When I was growing up, our president was a single mother with a background in the arts. No one thought it strange, and I think that has given Icelandic women so much in terms of believing that gender or circumstances don't have to hold you back.

WHERE DID YOU GRADUATE FROM, AND WHAT DID YOU DO NEXT?

I graduated from the Art Institute of California

in 2009. I came somewhat late to design, as I had already completed a degree in physiotherapy and worked in a clinic for a few years. Since graduation, my main focus has been on furniture and homeware. I was invited to participate in the Bernhardt Design Studio for young designers at ICFF 2010 in New York, and made my design debut at NeoCon 2011, when Coalesse launched my first commercial product, 'Sebastopol', a set of tables influenced by one of my favourite genres, Scandinavian design from the 1950s. It won the Best of NeoCon gold award, and was exhibited at the Salone del Mobile. Since then, I have worked on a number of interior-design projects, including a large office space, private residences and restaurants. At the moment, I am working on a line of modular shelves and a storage unit.

HOW DID YOU START OUT?

I loved the experience I had with 'Sebastopol' and Coalesse, and it gave me energy and the belief that I could design practical products that people and companies would like to buy. I had to take on a wide range of projects to sustain the business when first starting out, but I have always kept my focus on bringing the next viable product to the market. The process can be long, and there are days when I wonder if it was the right decision, but you have to keep faith, grab a good cup of coffee and your sketchbook, and look for inspiration.

BELOW 'Sebastopol' occasional tables, 2009

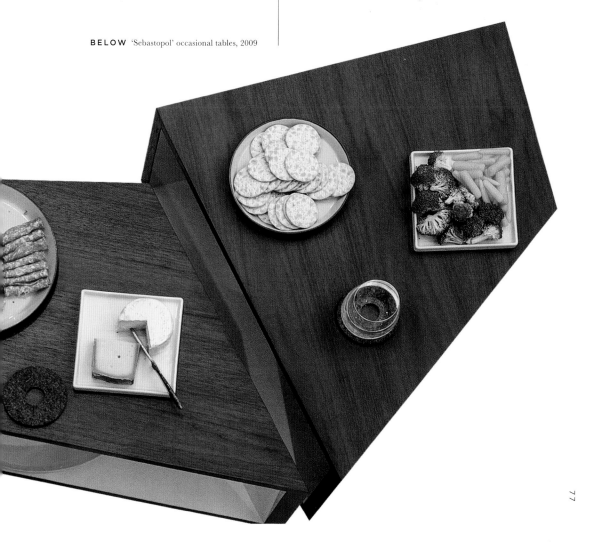

WHY DID YOU MOVE BACK TO ICELAND FROM THE UNITED STATES?

I lived in the US for six years and loved it, but we decided to move back to Iceland as we wanted to raise our children here. In the concept and prototype phases of a project, it can be very efficient to work here as people are so interconnected, and you quickly find the right collaborator, supplier or craftsman. When it comes to submitting ideas and meeting with companies, I need to travel to Europe or the US, as the local furniture production is rather small-scale. But being in between these key markets is also a great benefit.

WHO ARE THE NEW TALENTS TO WATCH?

In the last six to eight years there has been a huge awakening in the Icelandic design scene. Product design, fashion design, architecture and graphic design have all become much stronger and more visible. A big part of that has been the product designers graduating from the Icelandic Academy of Arts since 2004. The trade event DesignMarch has been going since 2009, and during it Reykjavik goes crazy for design and anything design-related. All of this helps create a strong community of designers who exchange ideas and come up with unexpected collaborations. We could do more to produce things at scale and export our designs, but we are getting there. There are a lot of talented designers here. A few I like are Dögg Guðmundsdóttir, Erla Sólveig Óskarsdóttir and the collective Vik Prjónsdóttir.

WHAT ARE YOUR MOST IMPORTANT SOURCES OF INSPIRATION?

The natural world has to be the strongest inspiration for my work. Having worked with the human body in my physiotherapy days, I am always amazed how the anatomy and function of the body can be a constant source of inspiration.

BYKATO

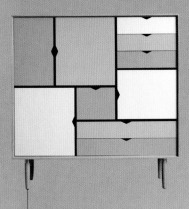

ABOVE 'S3' cabinet, 2014

RIGHT 'S1' sideboard, 2011

OVERLEAF 'Chicago' chair and 'Ultimate' sofa bed, 2011 (left); 'Madison' sofa, 2012 (right)

Karl Rossell and Tonny Glismand, the two creatives behind byKATO, have extensive experience in the furniture world. They were the recipients of the Wallpaper Design Award in 2012, and recently began working with the French branch of Habitat.

HOW DID YOU MEET?

We met at our former workplace, and realized that we could work very well together. Tonny worked in the furniture business for many years, while Karl took the academic route, studying architecture at the Royal Danish Academy of Fine Arts. These different experiences help us see things from more than one point of view in the design process.

WHO ARE THE MAIN DESIGNERS AND PRODUCERS YOU WORK WITH TODAY?

We have a very close relationship with Andersen Furniture, producers of quality Danish furniture. We also work with Tiger, for whom we designed a bicycle basket, and recently we began working with Habitat in France. So we are quite widespread in our design relationships.

IS DANISH DESIGN DIFFERENT FROM THAT OF OTHER COUNTRIES?

Danish design is about minimalism and functionality, and it is no longer exclusively Danish. There are several foreign designers working for Danish and other design companies, who use this style now. We are very much inspired by the long Danish design tradition, and over the years have come to realize how deeply rooted we are in it. We are also very inspired by our fellow designers around the world.

WHAT HAS BEEN YOUR GREATEST ACHIEVEMENT SO FAR?

Winning a Wallpaper Design Award 2012 for best dining table. We also think it's quite an achievement to be immortalized in this book about Scandinavian design.

DO YOU HAVE ANY FAVOURITE PLACES YOU LIKE TO VISIT?

We both love Copenhagen in the summertime. During those few months, nothing else comes close.

WHAT DOES NORDIC DESIGN TODAY REPRESENT TO YOU?

We are just very proud to be part of it.

BY LASSEN

Founded by two architects,
Mogens and Flemming Lassen,
this traditional Danish furniture
company has modernized its
structure, while continuing to
focus on the classics. It is still
owned by the family, including
Nadia Lassen, who explains the
success behind the family firm
and how it is planning to move
into the future.

THE COMPANY IS A FAMOUS OLD NAME. WHAT IS ITS BACKGROUND?

By Lassen owns the rights to the designs of two
of Denmark's greatest architects, Mogens and
Flemming Lassen, who received many awards for
their unique designs and iconic architecture. Today,
By Lassen is a family business, whose mission is to
carry the company legacy forward – because good
design lives on through new generations.

HOW DOES THE HISTORY OF BY LASSEN INSPIRE YOU?

We are very inspired by the Lassen brothers.
They were pioneers of Danish functionalism,
and it is fascinating to look back at what they did
and why they did it. They were not just designers,
they were also architects and designed houses and
buildings, as well as furniture and accessories.
I think we have such a great story to live up to,
and we owe it to the brothers to do our best.

HOW DID YOU MODERNIZE THE FIRM'S TRADITIONAL PRINCIPLES AND STYLE?

Most of our products are original Mogens and

ABOVE 'Frame' storage boxes

OPPOSITE 'ML42' stool, 1942, by Mogens Lassen

Flemming Lassen designs, but we also have a design team here, who develop the old sketches and finish them, if they were not finished originally. We also produce our own By Lassen designs, as well. For example, the 'Twin' table with a reversible tabletop was designed this year.

HOW DO YOU SEE THE DANISH DESIGN SCENE TODAY?

Danish design is classic, functional and aesthetic. Often the colours are delicate, or include wood or steel. The products are simple, without too many unnecessary details. Take the 'Kubus 1' candleholder, for example, which is functional and simple, without any ornate details. We have a strong tradition of design in Denmark, which, to me, is much stronger than that of our Nordic neighbours. The Danes spend most of their income on design, so it really matters to us.

TELL ME ABOUT YOUR COMPANY'S RECENT SUCCESSES.

The daily recognition means a lot to us. We follow social media very closely, and are proud every time someone tags 'By Lassen' on a picture. Our company has grown hugely over the past two years, from two to twelve employees. Without all of our followers, we couldn't have achieved that. Another achievement is the price achieved by Flemming Lassen's chair, 'The Tired Man', in 2014; it sold for €248,000, making it the most expensive chair ever sold at auction.

DO YOU HAVE ANY FAVOURITE PLACES IN SCANDINAVIA THAT INSPIRE YOU?

I have a lot of favourite places in Copenhagen, including the library of the Danish Museum of Art & Design, which holds wonderful exhibitions. For me, inspiration could also be found walking

through the gardens here in Copenhagen,
and being able to think surrounded by beautiful
trees and water.

**HOW DO YOU VIEW THE NEW NORDIC
DESIGNERS IN RELATION TO SUCH A
WELL-KNOWN COMPANY AS YOUR OWN?**
Nordic design today is to me very minimalist,
graphic and high on function. Often the materials
are a good quality, even if the object has been
mass-produced. I think that there are a lot of great
companies that focus on Nordic design, and it is
fantastic to see so many new designers succeeding.
The young designers give a modern edge to the
traditional Danish design classics, which I respect.

ABOVE 'Kubus' bowl, 1962, by Mogens
Lassen

OPPOSITE 'Kubus 1' candleholder, with
'Kubus' bowl

OLAFUR ELIASSON

Olafur Eliasson is well known internationally for his sculptures and large-scale installations. He represented Denmark at the 50th Venice Biennale, and has worked on a number of projects for Tate Modern in London, the Royal Danish Opera House and Louisiana Museum of Modern Art in Copenhagen, Louis Vuitton, and many others.

WHAT WAS IT LIKE GROWING UP IN TWO DIFFERENT COUNTRIES?
I was born in Denmark to Icelandic parents. When I was three, my father moved back to Iceland. I went to school in Denmark, but spent my time in Iceland during holidays and for extended periods living in and experiencing the countryside.

WHY DID YOU CHOOSE TO STUDY IN SCANDINAVIA, RATHER THAN ABROAD?
One of the things the programme at the Royal Danish Academy of Fine Arts offered was the opportunity to live in New York, where I worked as a studio assistant to the artist Christian Eckart. So I feel I benefited from formal training both inside and outside of Scandinavia.

WHAT DOES NORDIC DESIGN REPRESENT TO YOU?
Nordic design has the ability to touch you in both a physical and an ephemeral way. There is little exploitation that occurs in the production of Nordic design. It is not produced at the expense of our world, but made on behalf of society.

ABOVE 'Opera House' chandeliers, 2004

OPPOSITE Model room, 2010

WHY DID YOU DECIDE TO MOVE FROM SCANDINAVIA TO BERLIN?

I moved to Cologne in 1993 because I thought the art world was livelier there than in Copenhagen. During my time there, I visited Berlin occasionally and realized that the latter was actually more inspiring, and the work coming out of the city was more interesting. So after a year and a half, I moved to Berlin. It was a tough and very demanding place in the mid-1990s, but there was also such a high concentration of talented people.

TELL ME ABOUT THE LIGHT INSTALLATION YOU DESIGNED FOR THE DANISH OPERA HOUSE

I created the 'Opera House' chandeliers, three identical faceted spheres, for the foyer of the Royal Danish Opera House in Copenhagen in 2004. They are made out of a kind of glass that appears different according to how the light hits it – sometimes opaque, sometimes transparent, and in different colours. I've used this on a number of occasions, for the façades of the Harpa concert hall and conference centre in Reykjavik, for example. The spheres are lit from within by a series of small bulbs, and the combination of artificial and natural light creates a dynamic effect that depends on the position of the viewer. To get the full effect, you have to move around the work.

YOU FOUNDED THE SOCIAL ENTERPRISE LITTLE SUN. HOW DOES IT WORK?

Little Sun is a work of art in its own right. I set up it up in 2012, together with solar engineer Frederik Ottesen, to address the urgent need for energy and light for the 1.2 billion people around the world without adequate access to electricity. It is an ongoing project, and we have successfully distributed more than 85,000 solar lamps off-grid. The whole project actually began with a feeling: it came from a conversation we were having about being able to hold a piece of light in your hands, and that everyone should be able to experience what it feels like to hold sunlight. For me, it is the sense of empowerment the project offers that makes it art.

ARE THERE ANY NEW NORDIC DESIGNERS THAT YOU ARE INSPIRED BY?

The most interesting designers are the most experimental – designers who have not yet been exposed to the commercial market and been commodified by it. I am currently excited by the work of cross-disciplinary artists/designers such as Bjarke Ingels and Henrik Vibskov.

DAVID ERICSSON

Stockholm-based David Ericsson currently works in an interdisciplinary design studio with Marcus Berg. He has taken part in many successful exhibitions, including Frankfurt Ambiente 'Talents', and been featured in Vogue Living and Wallpaper magazines, as well as many books and galleries.

TELL ME ABOUT YOUR BACKGROUND

The David Ericsson Design Studio was founded in 2010 after graduation from Carl Malmsten Furniture Studies. For me, the current zeitgeist is important because we are living in a time of change. Everything just goes faster and faster, so we need to focus on the mood of the time to be able to develop good and interesting products. Our designs should not only suit the market for a short period of time; they should remain relevant for as long as possible and evolve over time to fit the new needs of our environment.

WHAT IS MOST IMPORTANT TO YOU IN YOUR WORK?

To find poetic ideas for the future, so we can combine historical and contemporary ways to find unexplored areas of design. Humour is an important ingredient that permeates my work.

WHO ARE YOU IN DAILY CONTACT WITH?

Since I'm a designer, I work with producers that deliver high-end furniture. I also work closely with master craftsmen to develop new ways of understanding the concept that surrounds us, the thing we called life; to make furniture that not only lasts for many lifetimes, but also puts things in a new context. I try to find the wrong materials and put them in the right place.

THESE PAGES 'Writing Desk', 2014, manufactured by Friends of Wood

IS SWEDISH DESIGN DIFFERENT FROM DESIGN IN OTHER COUNTRIES?

It isn't different anymore, because it is a global trend to use clean, slick design, natural materials, and so on. So we are all a part of it, even if some of us don't want to be.

WHAT DOES NORDIC DESIGN REPRESENT TO YOU TODAY?

Nordic design has become a global sales point, even the good Italian brands talk about Scandinavian style, and market themselves in a similar context. Perhaps Nordic design will continue to boom around the world, or perhaps it's about to die.

EVERYTHING ELEVATED

This Brooklyn-based design studio is run by two Norwegian designers, who both have experience working with leading companies around the world. Today they see Norwegian design from an international perspective, and focus on everything they can elevate, creating products such as tables, mirrors and wooden birds.

OPPOSITE, ABOVE 'Shorebird', 'Swan' and 'Ducky', all for Normann Copenhagen

OPPOSITE, BELOW Table from the 'Passivation Project', 2014

BELOW 'Midnight Sun' lamp, 2014

YOU DESIGN IN THE US, BUT ARE ORIGINALLY FROM NORWAY. HOW IS THAT DIFFERENT?

We like to think of it as gaining the best of both worlds. In Norway, we were trained in the Scandinavian design heritage, with its focus on a respect for material quality and honesty. In New York, we have collaborated with some of the biggest companies in the world, on everything from product development to installations, identity, brand strategy and engineering, which has given us a large professional network that enables us to work in a more multidisciplinary way, and to provide our colleagues with opportunities that used to only be obtainable for the largest companies out there.

WHAT DOES EVERYTHING ELEVATED CONSIST OF?

Currently, highly experienced Norwegian designers, educated in Oslo, Bergen, Lisbon and New York. Before joining forces, we worked for leading designers both in Norway and the US. Given our training and experience, we decided that we did not want to pursue solo careers with our names on the door, but rather combine our accumulated knowledge and set up a studio that could deliver

relevant strategic design services and grow into a company that focused on what we provide, not who is behind us.

WHO OR WHAT ARE YOU INSPIRED BY?

We are inspired by people and philosophy more than anything else. As designers, we appreciate beauty and developing new ideas, but in general, we try to look at the big picture to understand how all the pieces of the puzzle fit together and how we can elevate it.

DO YOU HAVE ANY FAVOURITE PLACES OF INSPIRATION IN SCANDINAVIA?

For us, it is very clear that the Scandinavian tradition of taking breaks to enjoy the outdoors and the simple life has some very important benefits. Taking a step back in order to let your mind reflect and contemplate gives important perspective to any problem-solving activity. Revisiting history is like unlocking a treasure chest of forgotten knowledge, and going to museums, such as the Henie-Onstad Art Centre in Høvikodden or the Norwegian Museum of Science and Technology in Oslo, can be great for actual inspiration and learning.

HOW DO YOU BEGIN THE PROCESS OF DEVELOPING A NEW PROJECT?

Staying informed about the past and everything that is going on is an important knowledge bank as we build our practice. For any project or collaboration, we invest in thorough research and analysis to make sure we find the right, although often hidden, potential. To us, design is only the final means of elevating

that strategic potential in the best way possible to create long-lasting value and design that will have a place in history.

HAVE ANY OTHER NORWEGIAN DESIGNERS INSPIRED YOUR WORK?

One of our favourite Norwegian architects is Todd Saunders, who is actually Canadian but based in Bergen. You can find his work all over the country. Perhaps the most impressive place we enjoy going to when we are home is his amazing lookout point in Aurland.

WHAT ARE THE CHALLENGES FACING THE NORWEGIAN DESIGN SCENE TODAY?

In a country with very little design production, it is clear that the big challenge for young designers is to find relevant collaborators and clients at home, which forces them to search for opportunities outside of Norway. As a lucky side effect, this has sparked a culture of collaboration between Norwegian designers, and to regard each other as colleagues, rather than competitors. This has, in many ways, helped the Norwegian design scene grow into what it is today. In the future, we believe that design will continue to expand outside the country's borders, but it is only a matter of time before someone has that great idea, which will rejuvenate the industry through utilizing the full potential of all those great designers at home.

OPPOSITE Mirror from the 'Passivation Project', 2014

BELOW Containers from the same project

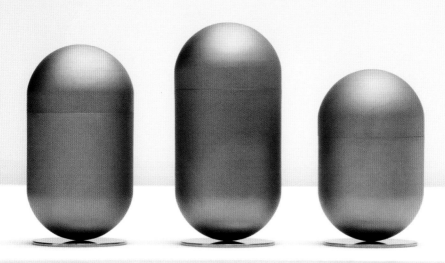

FÆRID

This design studio headed by Thorunn Hannesdóttir has been influenced by Iceland's storytelling heritage, and produces playful products that are available in over fifteen shops in Iceland. In 2014, Færid participated in the London furniture fair 100% Design.

THESE PAGES 'Berg' nest of tables

HOW DOES YOUR ICELANDIC UPBRINGING INFLUENCE YOUR DESIGNS?

Kids growing up in Iceland have a lot of freedom. When I was young, we spent most of our time outdoors – looking at fossils, collecting rocks, fishing and picking berries. During our travels in the summer, my dad would tell us folk tales, which was magical – those stories have stayed with me. We would also look at different rocks, and discuss what kind of lava formed them, and so on. I was a bit of a geek as a child, so I was really into all of this. I guess my choices of materials are influenced by my upbringing. I love to use high-quality materials in my products, and I always try to choose natural materials, or ones that I can connect in some way to Iceland. The memories I have from travels around the country inspire my designs. I loved creating things, in any shape or form, whether it was cooking, baking or building.

HOW DID YOU PROGRESS FROM BEING A STUDENT TO AN INDEPENDENT DESIGNER?

I studied art and design at the Technical College in Hafnarfjordur, near Reykjavik, and was really lucky to be able to study for my BA in product design at Central Saint Martins, London. After graduating in 2008, I moved back to Iceland and entered every design competition I could find. There were hardly any design jobs at the time, but I had always wanted to work in design, so giving up was not really an option. I worked without pay for start-ups, and helped out in any design-related job I could get. I worked as an intern for a young design firm in Iceland, which allowed me to do some pro-bono work organizing PechaKucha Nights for a few years – that was a fantastic experience. I got the chance to meet both international and Icelandic entrepreneurs, designers, architects and artists.

WHAT WAS IT LIKE SETTING UP A DESIGN STUDIO DURING THE FINANCIAL CRASH?

It was a bit of a fluke that we started the studio. I remember being at my sister's place in Iceland, scribbling down designs for the first products I sold (and am still selling). I invested about £500 in my first production, which seemed like a lot of money, especially for an unemployed designer with student loans. The packaging for the first two to three hundred pieces were hand-cut and packed by myself, my family and my boyfriend. After that, I was able to support myself by selling my designs, and so, along with two of my friends, Herborg Ingvarsdóttir and Karin Eriksson, I set up Færid. We had lots of ambition, took on high-risk projects that luckily paid off, and were fortunate to get good exposure quite soon, which pushed us to keep on going.

WHAT IS THE MANUFACTURING PROCESS LIKE IN ICELAND?

It is quite hard manufacturing modern design in Iceland because of how remote we are. We have quite a limited choice of manufacturers, and so we have to think outside the box when designing new products. It can be difficult to get international exposure, and sometimes hindering given how super-small the market in Iceland is. But designing here is anything but hindering. The energetic artistic community give me the motivation I need to grow and develop as a designer, and I wouldn't want to live anywhere else – at least, not at the moment. The manufacturers here are also very open to trying new things and working with designers. It's a win-win situation.

DO YOU HAVE ANY FAVOURITE ICELANDIC DESIGNERS?

There is a real awakening in Iceland in terms of design, and we have a diverse community of artists and designers. Some of my all-time favourite designs are by Thorkell G. Guðmundsson, my old teacher. I used to have a sofa bed designed by him as a child. One of Iceland's greatest sculptors is Ásgeir Sveinsson; he uses natural forms in different ways and adds amazing functions. His designs can be very multifunctional, perhaps why I tend to keep my own designs multifunctional. His energy also inspires me.

WHERE DO YOU SEEK NEW INSPIRATION FOR YOUR PRODUCTS?

My favourite source of inspiration is the discovery of small, everyday things. Sometimes when I am starting a project I like to go to the countryside, take photographs and sketch. I'm definitely more inclined to look to nature for inspiration. My cultural heritage has always inspired me and pushed me to work harder. I also love travelling, learning from other cultures and experiencing new and exciting things.

FRAMA

The designers behind Frama characterize their company as a 'work in progress'. Founder Niels Strøyer Christophersen explains that starting out without a collection, but having a deadline, can be a good motivator. In 2014, Frama won the Danish Design Award for Best Furniture.

HOW DID FRAMA START OUT?

Frama was established in 2011, when we took on an exhibition space at the Qubique furniture and design fair in Berlin without actually having a collection. But we rose to the challenge, and created a diverse collection of ceramic, wood, marble, cork and steel objects. By working intensively with designers, architects, typographers and photographers, we were able to realize within a few weeks the foundation of what Frama is today. We started out by focusing on solid materials with natural finishes and simple geometry – this now forms a strong part of our identity. We often refer to Frama as a third-generation design company. The first generation is formed by the companies of the 1950s, the golden age of Scandinavian design; the second by those established some years before the financial crash; and the third by us, representing those companies that came afterwards, with a completely different agenda and way of looking at furniture design, art, society, and values in general.

ABOVE 'Adam' stools, by Toke Lauridsen

OPPOSITE '9.5' chair, by B. Fex, and 'T1' table, by A/L/O

HOW DO YOU ENSURE YOUR DESIGNS HAVE A CONNECTION WITH EACH OTHER?

Since we work with different designers, architects and craftsmen, as well as creating our own designs, it is very important that each object is strong individually, as well as working together as a group or in context with other furniture in any given space. Our inspiration comes from art, buildings, urban spaces and the outdoors. We define our main interest in the creative field as a dialogue between two opposite poles: classic and contemporary approaches, digital and analogue production. Working in both worlds lends balance to our collections and our company.

HOW DO CHOOSE THE DESIGNERS THAT WORK FOR YOU?

We don't have a strategy as such in terms of who we work with. The key thing is the object, and whether it is interesting and fits our approach. From that point, the designers can be from anywhere in the world, with or without education in the field.

DO YOU SEE A DIFFERENCE BETWEEN DANISH DESIGN TODAY AND THAT OF OTHER COUNTRIES?

Since we have such a long history of modern design in comparison to other countries, it's difficult to talk about generalities. But overall, Danish design seems to focus on natural materials, and simple forms that have a strong communication to the user. Danish designers might be more comfortable in themselves than other designers from around the world trying to be the next Andy Warhol.

WHAT HAVE YOU FOUND THE MOST CHALLENGING WHEN CREATING A NEW COMPANY?

Being able to maintain our vision from the beginning, and not changing direction or strategy, focusing instead on our own DNA while constantly evolving. A good example is our latest collaboration with a Norwegian paint manufacturer, developing a blue-grey colour – St Pauls Blue – named after our new showroom, the former St Pauls Pharmacy, originally built in 1878.

IS THERE A GOOD PLACE TO EXPERIENCE DANISH DESIGN FIRST-HAND?

Visiting Ordrupgaard Museum, fifteen minutes by car outside Copenhagen, is a good experience because it's less crowded than the Louisiana Museum of Modern Art. It has a nice balance between historic and modern, with an international approach, but served up in a casual Danish way. The main building opened in 1900, and the contemporary addition, completed in 2005, was designed by Zaha Hadid (one of her best works, we feel). The two buildings stand in a nice contrast, but work very well together. Finn Juhl's (p. 24) is another of our favourite places.

WHAT DOES THE NEW NORDIC DESIGN REPRESENT TO YOU?

It represents an honest expression, using solid and true materials with a local production, where the manufacturing of the materials has a soul all the way to the end user, who is not afraid of receiving two pieces of wood that are not completely identical.

FUTUDESIGN

The speed of Finnish design studio Futudesign is difficult to keep up with. Their talents are widespread, and range from creating door handles to urban masterplans. They designed Bronda restaurant in Helsinki and an art hotel, and have their own city-planning programme on Finnish television.

OPPOSITE 'Ladyboy' pendant light at Farang restaurant, Stockholm, 2013

HOW DID FUTUDESIGN EVOLVE?

Futudesign is a young, Helsinki-based studio for architecture and design: cities, buildings, interiors, pop-ups and products. The story behind it is much older. A long time ago, years before Facebook and Twitter, there was an underground web forum for young designers and architects, mostly from the Helsinki area. The forum was anonymous and uncontrolled, anarchic and anti-establishment. The website was called Futudesign, the most idiotic name for a design office we could think of. Years went by, people moved on to other social media and web forums dried out. A group of like-minded designers from the 'Futuboard' needed a studio space, work started to roll in, and it was time to set up an office together. The choice of name was obvious.

ALTHOUGH INITIALLY ANTI-ESTABLISHMENT, YOU SEEM TO HAVE BECOME MORE MAINSTREAM. WHY?

Yes, we like new technology and programming, CNC routers, laser-cutters and 3D-printers, as well as natural materials, traditional building techniques and timeless beauty. We like steel structures, wet concrete and construction sites. We love timber, nail guns and circle saws. We like Swiss, Dutch and Danish architecture. We care about nature, yet don't believe that everything should be optimized. We like simplicity and (shared) luxury. Sometimes it's good to be boring, sometimes not. We like to be fast, efficient and precise. We are baffled by theory, yet are continually trying to get onto higher levels of abstraction. We know it's complicated. We like sailing, hiking and alpine skiing, hip-hop, art and Schlager music.

HOW DO YOU SEE DESIGN AND DESIGNERS TODAY?

Nowadays designers and tastes are quite similar all over the world. You have the same stuff in a hipster design/fashion store in Tokyo as in Helsinki. You don't have that many exotic local products. Same thing with architecture: no matter where you are, the story of locality is not valid anymore. You must have a much wider point of view, and see the audience or user from a different perspective.

HOW DO YOU FIND THE FINNISH DESIGN PROCESS DIFFERENT FROM THAT OF OTHER COUNTRIES?

Finnish designers often work alone or in super-small groups. They are skeptical about branding and marketing. Finnish designers are creative people; design itself is quite normal. In interviews, inspiration is always credited as coming from the natural world and the Finnish state of mind, but in reality we suspect that ideas come from Dezeen. We would like to work with a wide international network!

WHAT HAVE BEEN SOME OF YOUR HIGHLIGHTS?

The multidisciplinary combination of our office has led us to many great projects, including an art-hotel development in Helsinki with twenty of the coolest Finnish contemporary artists, and our own urban-planning show on Finnish television, *Kaupunki Uusiksi*. A bespoke pendant light for Farang restaurant in Stockholm: we needed a fixture that would provide an aesthetic bridge between the strong, structural presence of the restaurant space and the fine Asian cuisine. The result was 'Ladyboy', a spotlight that has both a slender grace and a sturdy masculine character.

GARBO INTERIORS

Swedish brand Garbo Interiors, formed by designers Anneli Ullman and Barbro Sahlin, is based in the Östermalm district of Stockholm, where they sell antiques and design inspired by the Gustavian period in the 1780s, along with pieces from the local Darlecarlia area. The firm also designs interiors for hotels and private homes.

OPPOSITE, ABOVE Interior of shop, featuring a wall of Farrow & Ball paint

OPPOSITE, BELOW Interior design for a private home

WHAT IS THE BACKGROUND OF THE COMPANY?

We started out in 2003 with a very small shop, selling reproductions of Gustavian furniture, produced in the south of Sweden. We are from the Darlecarlia neighbourhood of Stockholm, however, where there has been a tradition of craft production for centuries. Clients could hear from our accent that we came from there, and wanted to know if our furniture was from the area, as well. We began to produce our own furniture, inspired by the antiques made in Darlecarlia. After five years in our little shop, we were asked to design the interior of a hotel with one hundred rooms. We worked on the project full-time for three years, and had to sell our first shop. When we finished it, we founded our current shop where we have a much wider selection of goods and a space of almost 600m² (6,458 sq ft).

WHERE DO YOU FIND INSPIRATION FOR SOURCING ANTIQUES AND DESIGNING INTERIORS?

Our inspiration comes from what we find lovely and fresh ourselves, by visiting hotels and restaurants, and looking at magazines and books. We never visit the design fairs as we want to cater for other things not easily accessed through these channels. Our goal is to handpick unique items, as well as to produce them. Our motto is luxury is in raw materials, not gold and glitter. We use mainly linen, wood and handpainted furniture. Traditional Swedish handicraft is key in a lot of our products.

WHICH DESIGNERS OR PRODUCERS DO YOU WORK WITH?

We have worked with French Caravan, Ilse Crawford (p. 252), Köpenhamns Snickarna, and most importantly, the producers of our own products and the other handicrafts we sell, in which craftsmanship and Swedish production is important.

WHICH PROJECTS HAVE BEEN THE MOST SIGNIFICANT FOR YOU?

That three-year hotel project, from initial concept to completion and everything in between. That was a great learning experience. Also our pop-up shop in the Li Edelkoort Paris office, with our own cashmere collection.

GUBI

Established in 1967 in Copenhagen, Jacob Olsen, the son of the original founders, took the business to new heights by branching into concept stores and fashion. The company is based in an old tobacco factory, and is the recipient of several prestigious design awards. One of the company's chair designs is in the permanent collection of the Museum of Modern Art, New York.

WHAT IS THE BACKGROUND OF YOUR COMPANY?

Gubi was founded by my parents, Gubi and Lisbeth Olsen. I took over in 2001, and concentrated initially on the contract and office markets. In 2011, we launched a new strategy focusing on iconic designs, including our 'Bestlite' lighting collection from 1930 and the award-winning Gubi Chair Collection. Our aim was to bridge these two collections with designers from the twentieth century, who had the same spirit and understanding as the earlier masters.

HOW DO YOU CONNECT WITH YOUNG DESIGNERS TODAY?

We work with only a few young designers, as we find it very important that chemistry and a common understanding of design and business is maintained between the company and designers. We work with the Danish-Italian duo GamFratesi, and are about to launch a collection with German designer Sebastian Herkner. We are also reintroducing designs from our own heritage, including those by Greta Grossman and Kerstin Holmquist.

WHAT ARE YOUR THOUGHTS ABOUT DANISH DESIGN?

Danish design has a democratic yet aesthetic approach to design, as well as durable materials and a high level of functionality – both are very important parts of our heritage. It is simple, but with character, and, of course, wood is essential.

WHAT HAVE BEEN SOME OF THE MOST IMPORTANT MILESTONES?

Being Danish and coming from a country with so many great chair designs from the 1940s to the 1960s, the introduction of the 'Gubi' chair in 2003 was a very important step for our company. It was the first chair in our collection, as well as the first-ever chair produced with the new 3D veneer technique. It entered the permanent collection of

the Museum of Modern Art, New York, in 2004, and is now also in the collection of the Danish Museum of Art and Design. These are very important achievements for the company, as only a very few chairs designed after the golden age of Danish design in the 1950s and '60s have made their way into MoMA.

DO YOU HAVE A FAVOURITE PLACE IN COPENHAGEN?
I live close to the Danish Museum of Art and Design – that is my favourite place in Copenhagen. The library and changing exhibitions are always inspiring, but Copenhagen is a city with many great destinations for designs. We are very privileged.

THESE PAGES 'Grasshopper' lamp, by Greta Grossman, and 'Bonaparte' sofa

GUÐNÝ HAFSTEINSDÓTTIR

Guðný Hafsteinsdóttir's ceramic designs have been influenced by her studies at the Icelandic College of Art and Crafts, as well as by time spent working in Denmark, Finland and Hungary. She has participated in more than thirty exhibitions since 1996, and received several grants and awards for her work.

ARE YOUR DESIGNS INFLUENCED BY YOUR UPBRINGING IN ICELAND?

I was born and raised in the Westman Islands, and this experience of living near the sea with its fishing boats and rich birdlife has influenced, for example, my approach to a set of dinnerware for Mar, a restaurant in Reykjavik's old harbour area. My main inspiration was the ocean and wildlife, including the cormorant, from which the name, shape and colours of the set derives. The brown, orange and black all have multiple tones and harmonize with each other, and bear a resemblance to the volcanic rock and lava that Iceland, particularly the Westman Islands, is famous for.

WHAT PATH DID YOU FOLLOW TO REACH THE STAGE YOU'RE AT TODAY?

I trained to become a textiles and history teacher – that was my first university education. I then went on to make children's clothes for a few years, as well as teaching, but have been working with clay for the last nineteen years. Today, I divide my time between

OPPOSITE, ABOVE
Lamps for the 'Dance: Chandeliers, Lights and Lamps by Drifandi' exhibition, designed with Margret Gudnadóttir

OPPOSITE, BELOW
Vases for an exhibition at the Icelandic College of Art and Crafts

teaching and working in my studio. I believe my work is inspired by and reflects my educational background. My pieces often carry a historical and ethnic connotation.

WHY DID YOU DECIDE TO SET UP YOUR STUDIO IN ICELAND?

The year I graduated from art school I decided to open a gallery and studio, as I was incredibly excited and optimistic about the future. Two other ceramics graduates and I decided to do this together, which was necessary to be able to afford the ovens and equipment required. We slowly built up a well-equipped studio that has since grown; today I share it with seven other artists. We have worked here for the last nineteen years.

WHAT IS IT LIKE DESIGNING IN SUCH A REMOTE PLACE?

I don't feel as though Iceland is remote, partly because of the Internet and partly because flying to anywhere in Europe or the United States only takes a few hours. On the other hand, this is an island with very few inhabitants, so the market is small, with quite a distance from a large buyer's market. There are also very few factories that can manufacture design in Iceland, and none that can manufacture ceramic items. I have never been part of any other design community than the Icelandic one. I do like that everyone knows everyone else – people are close, which can provide both great support and competition.

HOW HAS THE HISTORY OF ICELANDIC DESIGN AFFECTED THE WORK OF TODAY?

That is a tough question, because design as a field in Iceland is very young, and it is less than ten years since it became possible to study product design and architecture here. Ceramics production in Iceland only goes back to 1946, so designers had

to get their education abroad, but this has led
to them bringing back trends and developments.
Together, the local design community owns and
runs the Iceland Design Centre. At the annual
DesignMarch festival, designers from different
associations participate and exhibitions are held
all over the city, with over a hundred events in the
programme. The festival has been a great education
for the public, and has brought design closer to
people and certainly enhanced their understanding
of what it is. As for my favourites, I would have to
name two architects: Högna Sigurðardóttir and
Manfreð Vilhjálmsson.

WHERE DO YOU GO FOR INSPIRATION?

My inspirations come from all over: my
surroundings, books, fashion, architecture and
the people around me. My students, too, are a
source of inspiration, because of their joyful
and disingenuous world view.

THESE PAGES 'Skarfur' series of bowls and vases

HAY

This popular Danish brand was launched in 2002 by Rolf Hay, now creative director, with a furniture collection at IMM Cologne. The company encourages young and well-established talent to create functional, affordable products. Hay won a Wallpaper Design Award 2014, along with over sixteen other awards to date.

WHAT WERE THE ORIGINS OF HAY?

Hay was founded with the aim of creating contemporary furniture with an eye on modern living and sophisticated industrial manufacturing. That remains our ambition today. Through our commitment to the design and production of furniture and accessories with an international appeal, we strive to make good design accessible to the largest possible audience. We are inspired by the structure of architecture and the dynamism of fashion, which we combine in durable, quality products that provide added value. Our vision is to keep creating straightforward, functional and aesthetic designs in cooperation with some of the world's most talented, curious and courageous designers. Our new co-brand – Wrong for Hay – launched its first collection during the London Design Festival 2013. The brand is spearheaded by British designer Sebastian Wrong, whose job is to nurture new design talent and develop cutting-edge products with his design team, and represents our desire to create a complementary, international brand with an eclectic, exotic and experimental design DNA as a natural reflection of Sebastian's base in London.

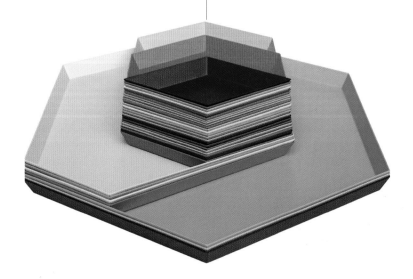

OPPOSITE 'Kaleido' tray,
by Clara von Zweigbergk

BELOW 'Copenhague' desk, by
Ronan and Erwan Bouroullec

OVERLEAF A selection of chairs
and tables, including the 'About a
Lounge Chair' design

DO YOU WORK WITH ANY INDEPENDENT DESIGNERS WHEN CREATING NEW PRODUCTS?

We work with a lot of designers, all of whom are extremely talented when it comes to designing and developing products, which means that we can take our collections to a whole new level. At the moment, we are working intensely with Stefan Diez and Ronan and Erwan Bouroullec – a dream come true, in both cases. Other designers we have worked with over the years include Clara von Zweigbergk, Hee Welling, Scholten & Baijings, Shane Schneck, among many others. We also work with a lot of newcomers, who may not have the same experience, but who have a certain entrepreneurial spirit.

WHY IS THERE SUCH A FOCUS ON SIMPLICITY IN SCANDINAVIAN HOMES?

In Denmark, and in Scandinavia generally, we spend a lot of time in our homes. We grew up with design traditions that make the younger generation very interested in creating a nice home. There has always been a lot of focus on materials, simplicity and everyday life.

WHAT DO YOU SEE AS YOUR MAIN ACHIEVEMENT IN THE DESIGN PROCESS?

There hasn't been a specific event that changed everything. In general, it is being able to design and develop high-quality products at a good price that is our main achievement. A new design is rooted in changes in society or the way we live – everyday life as it is today is our biggest inspiration.

HOW WOULD YOU DESCRIBE THE NEW NORDIC DESIGN TODAY?

Beautiful, functional items with a long life span, but that goes for most design. We work with designers from many different countries, not just Nordic ones, and we do not brand ourselves as being exclusively Danish or Nordic.

THESE PAGES 'New Order' shelving system, by Stefan Diez

HOTEL SP34

Owner Mette Brøchner-Mortensen of Brøchner Hotels has created an affordable design hotel right in the centre of Copenhagen. It features furniture by such Danish design legends as Hans J. Wegner and Nanna Ditzel, and has already been listed as a favourite in Wallpaper magazine.

WHAT IS THE BACKGROUND BEHIND YOUR BUSINESS?

Brøchner Hotels is a family-owned hotel chain, established by Bergliot and Hans Brøchner in 1982. The couple started with one small hotel, with fifty-three rooms. In the thirty-one years until 2013, they expanded the business to four hotels, and in 2014 our new boutique hotel – Hotel sp34 – opened with 118 rooms, conference facilities, a cinema, two à la carte restaurants, four bars and a rooftop terrace.

WHAT ARE YOUR KEY INSPIRATIONS?

We get our inspirations mainly from travelling, visiting other hotels, restaurants, museums and galleries, as well as from books and magazines. We are also true to the history and surroundings of the buildings we use, and took a lot of inspiration from the hotel's location on Sankt Peders Stræde, in Copenhagen's Latin Quarter.

WHO ARE THE MAIN DESIGNERS AND PRODUCERS YOU WORK WITH TODAY?

We work with architect Morten Hedegaard, but otherwise have no preference regarding

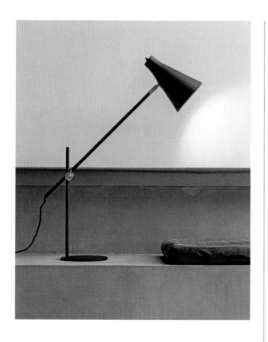

ABOVE 'Hunter' lamp, by Niclas Hoflin

OPPOSITE 'Cuba' chair, by Morten Gøttler

designers or products. Hotel sp34 includes designs by Danish legends including Hans J. Wegner, Nanna Ditzel, Niclas Hoflin and Inge Sommer – and even an old barn from Sweden. Producers that need to be mentioned include, among others, Carl Hansen, Hekabe Design, Rubn and Kabe.

HOW DOES DANISH DESIGN DIFFER FROM THAT OF OTHER COUNTRIES?

Danish design is simple and minimalist, with very clean lines. It is understated luxury. For example, apart from our conference chairs, all of the chairs we have in the hotel are made from wood. We believe Nordic design is the ultimate combination of simplicity and detail.

WHAT HAS BEEN YOUR GREATEST ACHIEVEMENT SO FAR?

Designing and launching Hotel sp34. We had a clear picture of what we wanted to achieve and we succeeded – it is a great achievement and we are extremely satisfied! The amount of interest the hotel has received from design enthusiasts, guests, partners and high-profile magazines has been overwhelming. Among many other fantastic results, Hotel sp34 was listed as one of the Ten Best Urban Hotels of 2014 by *Wallpaper* and *Time* magazines.

DO YOU HAVE ANY FAVOURITE PLACES IN SCANDINAVIA THAT INSPIRE YOU?

Stockholm is always a great place to visit – there are a lot of very well-designed restaurants and hotels. But a visit to the Danish countryside can also be very inspiring. One of my favourite places is Svinkløv Badehotel – understated luxury and great food. Berlin is also very inspiring, though it's not Scandinavia, but nearby.

WHAT DOES NORDIC DESIGN TODAY REPRESENT TO YOU?

To me, Nordic design represents our surroundings – wood, stone, ice, fur, and so on. We are true to our history. The colours are 'cold', the wood is warm, and the feeling is still cosy and homely. The simplicity, details and cosiness are what make Nordic design.

ABOVE Custom bed and lamps by Niclas Hoflin

OPPOSITE Furniture from Carl Hansen & Son, pendant light by Niclas Hoflin

HTL STOCKHOLM

This hotel in Stockholm was given the full Nordic design treatment by project architect Hanna Kucera Wengelin of Koncept Stockholm. Her client, HTL Hotels, plans to open twenty more hotels across Scandinavia over the next few years.

CAN YOU TELL ME ABOUT THE BACKGROUND OF THE DESIGN?

We put a lot of thought into what we believe the modern traveller looks for in a great hotel experience, and tried to remove everything that wasn't key to achieving that. The things we did keep were carefully chosen, focusing on every detail, along with form, quality and function. We wanted to create a calm and relaxing, as well as energizing, base for our guests.

WHAT WERE YOUR INSPIRATIONS WHEN DESIGNING THE HOTEL?

We looked to the world of fashion; early on in the project we settled on the tagline 'like a cashmere sweater with an edge'. It's about having a relaxed attitude towards quality, such as wearing trainers with a suit, or adding details from sportswear to evening wear. We wanted furniture that was smart and unfussy, and looked at basic geometric forms. Our designs were then realized with state-of-the-art materials and attention to detail.

WHAT DOES SWEDISH DESIGN MEAN TO YOU?

Sweden has a strong functionalist heritage: we design objects to be used. Swedes want things to be cosy and comfortable. We're interiors fanatics because we spend half of the year indoors.

ABOVE The quality of the design extends to the bathrooms

OPPOSITE A guest bedroom in the hotel

WHAT WAS YOUR APPROACH TO THE CHOICE OF FURNITURE AND INTERIORS?

Since we wanted this sporty, functionalist, fashion feeling to permeate throughout the hotel, we designed and chose furniture with simple lines, using 'techy' fabrics and graphics as an accent. Most of the furniture is custom-designed for HTL Hotels, which was both a brand-identity issue, as well as a means of achieving the look we wanted.

WHAT HAS BEEN YOUR GREATEST ACHIEVEMENT THIS FAR?

During the first four months, the hotel welcomed guests from eighty different nations, and has already taken the top spot for hotels in Stockholm on review sites such as Trip Advisor. Our guests' appreciation of the quality in the details and the design is echoed by the amount of reviews and mentions in social media that we have achieved in such a short space of time.

DO YOU HAVE ANY FAVOURITE PLACES IN SCANDINAVIA?

If you are visiting Stockholm, I would recommend a visit to contemporary art centre Magasin 3 or Fotografiska, for modern photography, both of which host ambitious and inspirational exhibitions. For magazines, I go to Papercut on Krukmakargatan – they have everything, including a great selection of films. I drink coffee at Johan & Nyström on Swedenborgsgatan; it was voted best Swedish café by the *White Guide* last year. If you venture outside Stockholm, the hotel Fabriken Furillen on Gotland is a magical place. Or visit Artilleriet in Gothenburg, which offers an interesting mix of furniture and design.

WHAT DOES NORDIC DESIGN TODAY REPRESENT TO YOU?

Nordic design has a strong identity. Over the last ten years or so, a new generation of Swedish architects and designers have emerged on the scene. They haven't left the functionalist heritage behind, but have updated it with a more refined aesthetic. Nowadays things can be both avant-garde and functional. These are exciting times for Nordic design across the whole of Scandinavia.

HUNTING & NARUD

London-based, Norwegian-born Amy Hunting and Oscar Narud have collaborated on projects for the Design Museum, in London, Wallpaper magazine and the Norwegian Design Council, and in 2013 designed the Fashion Scandinavia exhibition at Somerset House, London.

HOW DO YOU FIND BEING A DESIGN DUO FROM NORWAY, WORKING IN LONDON?

There's more competition in London – more people wanting to do the same thing – but that means there are more opportunities. It feels like the design field is broader, with different worlds within the larger design world. One example is design galleries, where limited-edition pieces are sold to collectors. This doesn't really exist in Norway.

Most of our work is not mass-produced, which allows us to explore other ways of making, and gives us the freedom to produce objects that would not be possible in a mass-produced way.

WHAT IS YOUR BACKGROUND?

We are both from Norway and studied in Denmark and London, before meeting in London. After working independently for years, we joined forces a couple of years ago and set up Hunting & Narud. Our work has changed since we started working together: it's suddenly a hybrid of the two of us and we really enjoy it.

HOW DO YOU FIND INSPIRATION FOR YOUR WORK?

'Inspiration' is a tricky word. It sounds so dreamy and romantic, when the reality is that the design process is a lot of hard work and dedication. We look at human behaviour, making

THESE PAGES 'Apex' tables, 2014

processes and materials, and how objects react to spaces as starting points in our work. We strive to create objects with a strong spatial impact.

DO YOU HAVE ANY FAVOURITE PLACES IN NORWAY OR SCANDINAVIA?

Living in another country really makes you appreciate such clichés as the landscape, the fjords and the mountains. We travelled around the west coast of Norway and were amazed by how stunning it was. We also love going to our cabin in the mountains to hide from the world for a little bit.

WHAT IS YOUR DESIGN PROCESS?

It usually starts with something that triggers our curiosity, which we then start investigating. There's a lot of thinking, discussing, drawing, making, failing, wanting to give up, desperation, feeling excited about it again, hating it, trying again and not giving up until we're both happy with the result.

ARE THERE ANY SCANDINAVIAN DESIGNERS THAT YOU ARE INSPIRED BY?

We don't really look to the design world for inspiration – that way everything ends up looking similar. But it's important to say that there is a really strong design community in Norway, where everyone is supportive and encouraging. We do group exhibitions and see each other at fairs and exhibitions, and get on very well.

HOW DO YOU SEE THE FUTURE OF NORWEGIAN DESIGN?

This is such an exciting time in Norwegian design – it seems as though it is growing in confidence and maturing. Not having an iconic design history is a blessing, as it means we can focus on the present, look forward and not dwell on the past.

KNEIP

Stian Korntved Ruud and Jørgen Platou Willumsen founded the Norwegian studio and workshop Kneip in 2014. They produce simple and handmade objects, with a focus on sustainability, materials and quality, and promote up-and-coming makers.

OPPOSITE, TOP ROW Making handmade leather pouches for products; 'Geometry' candlesticks, in pale pink and powder blue

OPPOSITE, BOTTOM ROW A selection of 'Geometry' candlesticks; the beginnings of a handmade wooden spoon

WHAT DOES NORWEGIAN DESIGN MEAN TO YOU?

We believe that Norwegian design stands out through its honest approach to creating objects with natural materials such as wood, textiles, leather and various metals. Norway's design history is rather short in comparison with our neighbours Sweden, Denmark and Finland, so in that sense we don't have too many unwritten or hidden rules to follow. It's also interesting that the leading design studios and designers in Norway are relatively young.

HOW DID YOU MEET?

We first met while studying for our degrees in product design. Since then we have shared a common interest in and fascination for music, art, design, objects and craft. It is the variety that makes us strong. By working in many different fields, our skills cover painting and electronic works, to simple interior objects.

ARE YOU, LIKE SO MANY OTHER NORWEGIAN DESIGNERS, INSPIRED BY THE OUTDOORS ?

I think we must say that the natural world is one of our biggest inspirations. But as we live and work in Oslo, the combination of urban living and the outdoors is an important contrast, and we find that many interesting ideas spring from the meeting of the two extremes.

HOW DOES YOUR DESIGN PROCESS WORK?

It's difficult to describe our design process, because it changes from project to project. What we have in common is that we are hands-on with the materials. It usually starts with collecting different types of materials, and storing them so that we can play with forms and shape to create objects. Sometimes we follow a function and then give it a shape, other times by craft, and often just out of an aesthetic point of view.

WHERE DO YOU THINK NORWEGIAN DESIGN IS HEADING?

It's hard to say, but it's really cool to see that Norwegian design does so well around the world, especially when conditions are so difficult. There are only a few furniture brands in Norway who dare to take a chance and use design in an innovative way. We have to seek out and work with brands in other countries.

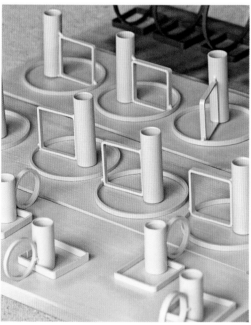

KRADS

Architectural studio Krads
was founded by two Icelandic
and two Danish architects:
Kristján Eggertsson, Kristján
Örn Kjartansson, Kristoffer
Juhl Bellman and Mads Bay
Møller. With studios in Iceland,
Denmark and New York, they
re-imagine Scandinavian culture
in globally aimed retail spaces,
restaurants and homes.

**HOW HAS YOUR UPBRINGING IN
ICELAND AFFECTED YOUR DESIGN?**
We believe our island is the best place on earth,
and that everybody here is somehow destined for
greatness – although this mindset also seems to lend
itself to a mild form of inferiority complex. There
is a certain creative drive here, and the belief that
anything is possible. Out of four partners, two of
us are from Iceland and two from Denmark, where
traditionally there has been a greater emphasis on
collective, rather than individual, achievements.
Our company has achieved a productive balance
between these two polarities.

THESE PAGES 'Stöðin' roadside stop,
Borgarnes, 2012

WHAT DID YOU DO BEFORE SETTING UP KRADS?

All four of us studied architecture at Aarhus School of Architecture, but did our internships in different places: Los Angeles, Prague, Rotterdam, as well as Aarhus. During our studies, we collaborated on a number of architectural competitions and continued to do so after graduating. We gained experience by working for two or three years for such well-known Danish practices as 3XN, Schmidt Hammer Lassen and AART Architects, before setting up on our own.

WHY DID YOU DECIDE TO ESTABLISH YOUR OWN COMPANY?

The dream was born during our time at architecture school, and the opportunity to realize it came in 2006, when we won first prize in a competition to design a retail space in Iceland. With strong ties to Iceland and Denmark, we opened studios in both countries simultaneously, and have continued to operate in the two places ever since. For most architects in Scandinavia, winning a competition is the only way to start your own practice. It is a narrow opening into a field we feel lucky to be a part of.

WHAT IS IT LIKE TO CREATE MODERN DESIGN IN SUCH A REMOTE PLACE?

There is a certain sense of isolation in the geographic reality of Iceland: one island in the middle of the Atlantic Ocean. Most of the time, however, it doesn't feel as if we are remote. Our Reykjavik office is conveniently located between Europe and North America. In our globalized and technology driven society, Iceland feels less isolated and more like a hub between the two continents.

TELL ME ABOUT DESIGNING STÖÐIN

Icelandic culture is in many ways shaped by American influences, owing to the sixty-five-year presence of an American army base here. The project addresses this complex relationship, referencing the American diner and contrasting it with the local building method of cast concrete. The exposed concrete of the exterior gives the diner a permanence its American counterparts traditionally don't have. The semicircular restaurant inside the building offers panoramic views of the Borgarfjörður fjord, while the curvilinear form allows for the smooth circulation of cars outside.

WHAT CHARACTERIZES THE ICELANDIC DESIGN SCENE?

Because Icelandic architects have always had to travel abroad to gain their degrees, they have already engaged with the wider architectural scene, resulting in diverse international influences on local practices. As urbanization only began in the early twentieth century (until then, the population lived largely in turf houses), our architectural history is very young, compared with that of most western countries. So there is a continuing emphasis on defining what constitutes the country's architectural identity.

WHERE DO YOU GO FOR INSPIRATION BEFORE STARTING A NEW PROJECT?

A trip to one of the communal baths always helps, but projects usually provide plenty of inspiration on their own. In our approach, the aesthetics follow a careful reading of each one's functional, cultural and geographical framework. A thorough understanding of the requirements of each task includes identifying core issues and challenges as a way of revealing its potential. This becomes the foundation of generating a strong vision.

JOANNA LAAJISTO

After spending over eight years in the US working for a large international architectural firm, interior designer Joanna Laajisto decided to make her mark on the retail scene in Helsinki. She has since created successful spaces inspired by New York and Amsterdam, while remaining true to her favourite source of inspiration: Finland's great outdoors.

WHAT IS THE BACKGROUND OF YOUR STUDIO?

I founded it after I moved back home to Helsinki in 2009, after spending eight years on the West Coast of America. I had been studying to become an interior architect, as well as working for an architectural firm in Los Angeles. The studio focuses on designing commercial spaces, including restaurants, retail and workplace environments.

WHAT MOTIVATES YOU?

My work is driven simultaneously by functionality and aesthetics. A space needs to function well, but, more importantly, to evoke feelings. I try to spend a lot of time in a space to sense the mood it should have before working out what it should look like. I like places that have a soul. It can be ultra-modern or very old, as long as it feels like it has always been that way. I also get a lot of my inspiration from travelling. I love big cities such as New York, London and Paris. I just came back from Amsterdam, which is also a great city.

THESE PAGES Intro restaurant and nightclub, Kuopio

WHAT DOES FINNISH DESIGN MEAN TO YOU?

It is minimalist and functional. Each piece has to have a purpose in the space. We are very practical here, so my personal designs are also very practical. I never just decorate. But with that said, I also try to add warmth and layers to the designs, so that they are not cold and sterile, as some Finnish design in its purest form can be.

WHAT IS YOUR DESIGNING PROCESS LIKE?

My biggest mission as a designer is to slow down the fast pace at which design ages today. This has a lot to do with blogs and social media. Design becomes like fast food: disposable. People get bored quickly, because they keep seeing the same things. They get the urge to continually change their environments and buy new things, which is not very eco-friendly. I want to design objects and spaces that last, and are classic enough to be timeless. You need to get past the trends, but still stay current and interesting. This is the key driver of our design philosophy.

WHAT HAS BEEN YOUR GREATEST ACHIEVEMENT SO FAR?

That we have been able to create financially and socially successful concepts – not just pretty places – for our clients. One of my missions when returning from the US was to make Helsinki a bit more lively and interesting for both residents and tourists. By being able to design environments for our retail and restaurant clients, we have been able to do that. One project at a time, it makes me feel that there is a greater meaning to what we do.

DO YOU HAVE ANY FAVOURITE PLACES IN FINLAND?

Definitely the outdoors. I need to be surrounded by nature regularly; it is the only way I can really clear my head. I spend a lot of time in the Finnish archipelago with my family. But I also love just hiking in the forest and cooking on the campfire.

WHAT DOES NORDIC DESIGN TODAY MEAN TO YOU?

Local craftsmanship, honest materials, ecological values and an ethical way of thinking.

LITH LITH LUNDIN

This furniture company is based in the small village of Torsåker, Sweden. Erik Lith, Martin Lith and Hannes Lundin set it up as a reaction against mass-consumerism, and to provide handmade objects that emphasize craftsmanship. Their work has been shown at Tent London, and in the exhibitions 'French Design Connection' in New York, and 'In Real Life' at the Salone del Mobile.

WHAT IS THE CONCEPT BEHIND LITH LITH LUNDIN?

The company is the result of a thesis by Erik Lith and Hannes Lundin while students at Carl Malmsten Furniture Studies about sustainable furniture production within a 50km (31-mile) radius. This idea later formed the basis of our company. As we design and manufacture by ourselves, we have not developed many collaborations with other designers.

HOW DO YOU GO ABOUT PRODUCING YOUR FURNITURE DESIGNS?

When we designed 'Glimm', 'Seven' and 'Dome', we looked at the structural principle of tensegrity, in which the tension and pressure between materials frame the construction. For our latest chair, 'Will', we worked with green wood and woodworking techniques. We dry the assembled chair, allowing the shrinkage in the wood to shape the finished piece. The natural tensions in the wood make each chair unique.

ABOVE The 'Will' chair

OPPOSITE The 'Seven' stool

WHAT IS YOUR DEFINITION OF SWEDISH DESIGN?

It's hard to say how Swedish design differs from that of other countries, as the design scene differs so widely within Sweden itself. Simplicity and a cleanness of line are usually given as characteristics of Scandinavian design, and we think that's a pretty accurate description.

WHAT ARE YOU PROUDEST OF ACHIEVING?

The way we work, and the fact that we never give up. For example, we had the idea of making our own egg and oil tempera to stain the furniture with. We began by sowing our own field of flax to make linseed oil, and tearing up old pine roots to make pigment. After harvesting, clearing and pressing the linseeds and cutting, drying and burning the pine roots, we could start experimenting to find the best stain.

IS THERE A PARTICULAR INSPIRATION BEHIND YOUR FURNITURE DESIGNS?

This is a hard question. The inspiration for our work comes from both sweaty nightclubs in Gothenburg and working on the farm. As the ideas for our designs usually develop very slowly, it's hard to pinpoint one particular inspiration. It's the mixture between city life and the serenity of the countryside that inspires us the most.

WHAT DOES NORDIC DESIGN TODAY REPRESENT TO YOU?

Nordic design is about form and function, closely interconnected. Minimalist and straightforward design, with the user and function always in mind.

LEFT TO RIGHT 'Dome', 'Seven' and 'Glimm' stools

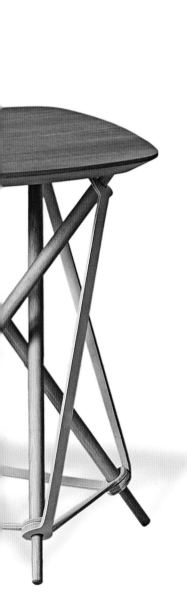

CECILIE MANZ

After studying at the Royal Danish Academy of Fine Arts and the University of Art and Design Helsinki, Cecilie Manz founded her own studio in 1998. Her work has been shown at the Miyake Design Studio, Vitra Design Museum, Alvar Aalto Academy and the Danish Museum of Art and Design, and she has been the recipient of awards including the Finn Juhl Prize 2007, Kunstpreis Berlin 2008, Bruno Mathsson Prize 2009 and the Crown Prince Couple's Award 2014.

WHAT IS THE BACKGROUND OF YOUR COMPANY?

I studied to be a furniture designer, and set up my own studio immediately after leaving the Royal Danish Academy of Fine Arts. I work in the fields of furniture, lighting and industrial design, and produce limited editions and one-off pieces. I enjoy these two strands equally: commissioned collaborations with companies based around an industrial developed product, and experimental free work without boundaries.

WHAT ARE YOUR KEY INSPIRATIONS?

My own life is a very important source of inspiration. When solving a problem or giving

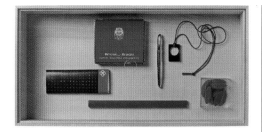

ABOVE 'Treasure Box', 2003, manufactured by Mooment

OPPOSITE 'Beolit12', 2012, produced by B&O Play

RIGHT 'Spectra' vases, 2007,
manufactured by Holmegaard

OPPOSITE 'Minuscule' chair,
2012, manufactured by Fritz Hansen

shape to something, it's crucial to relate to the
situation. How would you use the object yourself?
Would you place it in your own living room?
Often the task itself holds the key, and thus the
solution. Plus, of course, some hard work.

**WHO ARE THE DESIGNERS AND
PRODUCERS YOU WORK WITH TODAY?**
I work with manufacturers in many different
fields – furniture, lighting, textile, glass, ceramics –
mostly from Scandinavia, but also Germany
and Japan.

**HOW DOES DANISH DESIGN DIFFER
FROM THAT OF OTHER COUNTRIES?**
I think Danish design is all about details and
using the right material in the right place, as
well as craftsmanship. It's a lot of hard work,
on top of passion.

**WHAT DOES NORDIC DESIGN TODAY
REPRESENT TO YOU?**
Perhaps it's slowly finding itself again after
the 'golden age', hopefully in a new way,
so that we avoid an embarrassing pastiche.

MISS CLARA

One of Stockholm's most celebrated Jugendstil buildings has been transformed into the exclusive boutique hotel Miss Clara under the direction of CEO and owner of the Nobis Group, Alessandro Catenacci. He is also the driving force behind many of Stockholm's top restaurants and hotels.

WHAT WERE YOUR THOUGHTS BEHIND THE DESIGN OF MISS CLARA?

The design originated from a collaboration between the Nobis Group and Gert Wingårdh Architects. The aim was to transform an old girls' school in central Stockholm into a modern hotel with a world-class restaurant and bar. It is one of the best-preserved Jugendstil buildings in Stockholm, and after a number of meetings with the team to define the project's direction, the design work started.

WHAT WERE THE KEY INSPIRATIONS?

A key inspiration was, of course, the old school, but also the result of many discussions around what is the role and function in a hotel. What does the integrity of the guests mean during the daily running of the hotel?

WHAT WAS BEHIND THE APPROACH TO THE INTERIOR DESIGN AND CHOICE OF FURNITURE?

We want our hotels to be fresh and current in a timeless way, over long periods. To achieve this, it is necessary to choose materials and furniture that will last and age well, such as leather, stone, wood, limestone, and bentwood chairs and tables.

WHAT HAS BEEN YOUR GREATEST ACHIEVEMENT THIS FAR?

One of our proudest achievements has been creating the warm and inviting character of Miss Clara. We have an amazing workforce at the hotel, who bring a genuine personality that creates an unbeatable atmosphere. You feel the energy, built on dedication and love for the hotel.

DO YOU HAVE ANY FAVOURITE PLACES IN SCANDINAVIA THAT INSPIRE YOU?

Actually, we think it is more interesting to go a little bit further – to Germany or the UK. Berlin is a never-ending source of inspiration, as are London and Hamburg.

WHAT DOES NORDIC DESIGN TODAY REPRESENT TO YOU?

I think you can say that Nordic design in general stands for well-lit interiors, well-designed furniture and textiles, and many young photographers and designers. We like to work with designers who can develop a design from the existing conditions, rather than going with the flow.

MUUTO

Although 'muuto' is Finnish for new perspective, the company is based in Copenhagen and was founded by two Danes to handpick the brightest new talents and give them free rein to venture beyond the Scandinavian design tradition. Head designer Nina Bruun discusses her love of the outdoors and her native city as the inspirations behind the new Muuto collection.

WHAT WAS THE IMPETUS BEHIND STARTING UP A NEW DESIGN COMPANY?

Muuto was founded in 2006 by Peter Bonnén and Kristian Byrge, who were driven by a desire to add a new perspective with their choice of product offerings. Their aim was to set the highest standards in terms of quality, the finest design, working with the best designers, and so on. The company started out by offering accessories and lighting design, and has had a global outlook from the outset. We are very much in tune with our Scandinavian design heritage, and want to export our objects to wherever in the world there is a desire for them.

WHAT IS THE TRADEMARK OF MUUTO?

The Scandinavian tradition of creating long-lasting design, in terms of both function and aesthetics, focusing on quality and detail orientation, with all the elements of a given design there for a reason. It's in our genes and provides our foundation. We stand on the shoulders of our design history, and aim to reinvigorate that heritage by adding a new chapter. This is what we term 'New Nordic'.

ABOVE 'Elevated' vase, by Thomas Benzen

OPPOSITE 'Split' table, by Staffan Holm, 'Nerd' chairs by David Geckeler

HOW DO YOU CHOOSE NEW DESIGNERS TO COLLABORATE WITH?

Working with a range of designers is a key part of what we do. In this way, we make sure that Muuto products are always fresh and full of new ideas. We choose designers who are committed to our way of thinking, and can offer the look and feel we are aiming for.

HOW DOES DANISH DESIGN DIFFER FROM THAT OF OTHER COUNTRIES?

I believe that Danish design appeals to many people, as it can be novel and exciting in so many ways, and yet continues the traditions that have become so fundamentally Scandinavian over the years. Items are functional, honest and produced to the highest standards of quality and craftsmanship. The aesthetics are simple and inviting, and our egalitarian approach aims to produce design that is affordable and provides value for money.

DO YOU HAVE ANY STAND-OUT MOMENTS IN THE HISTORY OF MUUTO?

There have been many high points in our history so far. Every time a new item is released is a great achievement for us, as it is the culmination of a long process of discovery in the development and design phases. Each product is a labour of love in the pursuit of craftsmanship, quality and thoughtfulness.

RIGHT A series of 'Cover' chairs, by Thomas Benzen

PREVIOUS PAGES 'Soft Blocks' sofa, by Petter Skogstad

WHERE DO YOU GET YOUR INSPIRATION FROM WHEN DESIGNING NEW PRODUCTS?

I love the outdoors, and living so close to it here in Copenhagen provides an endless source of creative inspiration. As nature is constantly in flux, colours, patterns and textures are constantly changing and continually inspiring. I love the North Sea coastline in Denmark, and the woods and skerries of Sweden.

WHAT DOES NORDIC DESIGN TODAY MEAN TO YOU?

For us, Nordic design means 'New Nordic', which is all about adding a new chapter – essentially building on our design heritage, which we combine with the forward-thinking ambition of adding new perspectives by working with new materials, techniques and ideas, conceptual thinking and the best contemporary designers. A good example is our 'Cover' chair. The starting point was a typical Scandinavian armchair, but by taking a 'New Nordic' approach, we added a thin, pressed plywood wraparound veneer, which not only functions as a comfortable armrest, but is also the mechanism that holds the chair together. 'New Nordic' also means that the Scandinavian mindset remains central in our founding principles. We produce democratic, social (as opposed to individual), affordable luxury. We want everyone to be able to afford our designs.

DITTE BUUS NIELSEN

One of the up-and-coming talents in product design, Ditte Buus Nielsen has already won two awards in Denmark, and taken part in two exhibitions. She graduated with an M.Arch from Aalborg University, and has produced designs for Gubi (p. 112), Ikea and design consultancy VE2.

OPPOSITE, ABOVE 'Bend' lamp, 2015, launched by Bent Hansen

OPPOSITE, BELOW 'Curv' daybed, designed with Anders Dancker-Jensen

WHY DID YOU WANT TO START OUT ON YOUR OWN?

I began as an independent designer, because I wanted to carry out my ideas into real projects. I find it interesting to combine different functions and solve everyday problems with simple, playful aesthetics, and I believe my ideas can fit into many people's homes. Today, I'm happy to work with Trip Trap, Bent Hansen and Bolia.

WHERE DOES THE INSPIRATION FOR YOUR PRODUCTS COME FROM?

Many things inspire me. I find inspiration in everyday living conditions and living in small spaces, and at flea markets and vintage stores, where I often stumble across interesting details in forgotten objects.

WHAT IS THE DIFFERENCE BETWEEN DANISH AND INTERNATIONAL DESIGN?

This is easy: understandable design with great functionality. Danish design is simple but interesting, and is designed with quality in mind. I also see Danish design today as a tribute to the great architects of the past, but with a new perspective and the will to look forward. It is exciting to consider how the Danish design scene will look like in the future.

WHAT HAS BEEN YOUR GREATEST ACHIEVEMENT SO FAR?

Winning the Bolia Design Award 2014 with my multifunctional room-divider, 'Hedge'.

HOW DO YOU MARRY YOUR PRODUCTS WITH THE NORDIC WAY OF LIFE?

As an example, I was on a road trip through the Norwegian landscape this summer, which created a lot of ideas for new projects. I live in the northern part of Denmark but enjoy visiting Copenhagen, a city constantly on the move, and spending Sundays visiting museums. The juxtaposition of city life and rural retreats sparks ideas about combining materials in new ways. How we live inspires me. But I also get inspired when I least expect it.

WHAT DOES THE NEW NORDIC DESIGN MEAN TO YOU AS A DESIGNER?

It is about quality and an appreciation for materials. Nordic design is not loud in its presence, but the simplicity and eye for detail is loud and the longer we are surrounded by simplicity, the more we enjoy it.

NIKARI

One of the great old furniture companies of Finland, Nikari, founded in 1967, is known for the exquisite quality of its designs and for having worked with such names as Alvar Aalto and Kaj Franck. It is based in a small village, in the oldest machinery workshop in the country. Licensed manufacturing of its designs began in Kyoto in 2010.

WHAT IS THE HISTORY OF YOUR COMPANY?

Nikari is a manufacturer of sustainable wood furniture and custom-made furnishings for both public buildings and private homes. The founder – master cabinet-maker Kari Virtanen – has worked with the great Finnish architects and designers, and over the years has maintained his focus on wood and its ecological benefits. Today Nikari is owned and run by the next generation. After decades working mainly inside Finland, the new owners have taken Nikari's philosophy and ideology abroad. The company collaborates with designers from around the world and the collection keeps evolving. The studio workshop is located in the village of Fiskars, in southwest Finland, in the oldest machinery workshop in the country.

WHAT ARE THE MOST IMPORTANT ASPECTS YOU ARE TAKING INTO THE FUTURE?

The company philosophy combines traditional craft methods with timeless design, resulting in an ultra-modern way of working and living sustainably in today's world. The basic components of our vision include no compromise in quality, whether functional, aesthetic or technical, and using local wood from sustainably grown forests. It also emphasizes making every detail count in high-quality craftsmanship and using ecological surface-treatment materials.

WHAT DOES DESIGN MEAN TO YOU?

Designing today means so many different things that it is difficult to give an answer. For us, it means respecting the character and requirements of the wood we use in our designs. We try to create forms that feel natural and are easy to touch and use.

HOW DOES FINNISH DESIGN DIFFER FROM THAT OF OTHER COUNTRIES?

All modern Nordic design styles are light and simple, so the differences are not easy to spot. Finnish design often seems to be a bit more rough and ready, yet at the same time durable and functional. At Nikari, the idea is to not let the wood feel 'dead' through too much surface treatment. We have a saying, 'every product should have a soul', and we believe that, in the end, people will always love something beautiful.

OPPOSITE 'August' stool, by Aamu Song and Johan Olin

BELOW 'July' table/stools, by Nao Tamura

IS THERE ANYONE YOU WERE ESPECIALLY HAPPY TO WORK WITH?

It is impossible to say – we are grateful for everything we have the opportunity to do. It has been wonderful to work with different people – true talents in their fields – from all over the world. We have awards and products in the permanent collections of design museums and museums of modern art, which is also special. Hopefully, we will always feel that we are achieving something new and worthwhile every day.

DO YOU HAVE ANY FAVOURITE PLACES IN SCANDINAVIA THAT INSPIRE YOU?

Our own village, Fiskars, is very dear to us, and is a real creative centre with craftsmen, designers and artists. We have fantastic exhibitions, events and parties there. It is also a big plus to have the best Finnish forests and scenery on your doorstep. Our workshop is an idyllic place to work in, with all of its history. But there are so many places all over the world one can be inspired by – buzzing cities, beautiful beaches. There are many different ways to get inspired. In Scandinavia, the mountains and fjords of Norway are breathtaking; the archipelago of Turku, Åland and Stockholm must rank among the most beautiful in the world; Copenhagen and the Tivoli in the autumn, especially Halloween; Helsinki and its beaches in summertime . . . The list could go on and on.

WHAT DOES NORDIC DESIGN TODAY REPRESENT TO YOU?

Functionality, pale colours and light materials, simple, easy-to-use forms, durability and a beautiful modern lifestyle – at home and at work.

LEFT TO RIGHT
'Café Basic Tnt3' chair, 2009, by Tomoshi Nagano; 'Café Basic JRP3' chair, 2014, by Jenni Roininen; 'Seminar TT2' step ladder, 2005, by Kari Virtanen; 'Café Basic JRV1' LED light, 2014, by Jenni Roininen; 'Café Classic RMJ1-2-3' stool, 1999, by Rudi Merz

NORMANN COPENHAGEN

Paul Madsen and co-founder Jan Andersen believe in working with established designers and new talents from around the world. Named by The New York Times as one of its Twelve Treasures of Europe, Normann Copenhagen has won several awards, and their iconic washing-up bowl is used in the restaurant of the Museum of Modern Art, New York.

HOW DID NORMANN COPENHAGEN COME ABOUT?

Before setting up Normann Copenhagen in 1999, we had each been running our own company for a couple of years. We kept running into each other at trade shows and quickly realized that we had similar interests and values, as well as sharing a passion for design and a desire to bring something new and unexpected into the world of design, so we decided to team up. The first product we launched was the 'Norm 69' lamp, which quickly became a bestseller for us. Over the years, we put several other products on the market, and today the collection consists of a wide range of furniture, home accessories, textiles and lighting.

HOW DO YOU DESIGN NEW PRODUCTS?

We choose products that we think bring something new and, hopefully, unexpected to the world of design. It can be a new shape, an added function or a reinterpretation of a product. We don't just launch a product according to its type or what we think is missing in our collection. It has to be the right product, something that we look at and think, this is special and something we haven't seen before. This approach means that our products are all

OPPOSITE 'Era' lounge chair and 'Stay' table, with a 'Cap' table lamp

BELOW 'Ekko' throws, on top of a 'Box' table in turquoise

designs that we believe in and reflect our personal tastes and views. When we choose colours for our products and style the photograph, we are often inspired by the fashion world, but the designers we work with get their inspiration from lots of different places. We like that our products aren't always inspired by the same things. We think it helps make each design unique.

DO YOU WORK WITH UP-AND-COMING TALENT OR ESTABLISHED DESIGNERS?

From the very beginning, we have collaborated with both new and established designers from around the world, and continue to do so today. We set up a design studio with a young team of creative and highly skilled designers, who create high-quality designs that span the fields of craft and industry. Simon Legald, a Dane, has worked with us in the studio as Senior Designer since he graduated in 2012. Apart from our own design team, we have worked with Danish designers Nicholai Wiig Hansen, Ole Jensen and Iskos-Berlin; Swedish designer Jonas Wagell; German design studio Ding3000; Dutch designer Marcel Wanders; Australian designer Adam Goodrum and Norwegian designer Lars Beller Fjetland (p. 64).

HOW DOES DANISH DESIGN DIFFER FROM THAT OF OTHER COUNTRIES?

Scandinavian design is generally very minimalist, with clean lines and light wood such as ash, birch and oak characterize it. Denmark has a history of great design, which we take great pride

in. The Danish design scene flourished in the 1950s and '60s, when many of the iconic designs were conceived. Then and now, Danish design is characterized by its simplicity, functionality and high quality. Today, we see a broader, more experimental, even playful, design scene. Our products have a minimalist aesthetic characteristic of Scandinavian design, but they are also colourful, humorous and eye-catching.

WHAT HAS BEEN YOUR GREATEST ACHIEVEMENT THUS FAR?

That's a difficult one. There are many events in our brand's history that I will remember. For the last couple of years, we have focused on developing our furniture range, and we now have a collection that can cover every room in the home. We are receiving great feedback on the designs from both our customers and the end consumers, and we are thrilled that we have already won awards for some of the furniture pieces, such as the German Design Award for the 'Era' lounge chair and the Interior Innovation Award for 'My Chair' and the 'Just Chair'. It is always nice to be recognized for the work you do. Until now, we have been known primarily for home accessories, but now we are a bona-fide furniture company and one of the leading design brands in Scandinavia. That is a position we are greatly honoured to hold, and an achievement we are proud of every single day.

DO YOU HAVE ANY FAVOURITE PLACES IN SCANDINAVIA THAT INSPIRE YOU?

Our company is based in Copenhagen, and the city is very special to us. Although Copenhagen is small, it has a vibrant cultural life, world-class restaurants and excellent design. I love dining at Restaurant Kul, in the meatpacking district. The food is cooked on a big open grill, and the flavours are always intense and experimental. I also enjoy taking a trip up north to visit the Louisiana Museum of Modern Art, in Humlebæk. It is near the coast, and has beautiful views over the sea. If you enjoy architecture, the building itself makes the trip worthwhile, and the atmosphere is calming and stimulating at the same time. Our flagship store, located at the heart of the Østerbro in Copenhagen, is also a great place to visit. Our goal was to create an innovative and inspirational space for customers. Along with our own products, the store sells furniture, lighting, music, fashion, perfume and home accessories.

WHAT DOES NORDIC DESIGN TODAY REPRESENT TO YOU?

The old design classics have been a great foundation for a long time, but I think we need to create new designs that can become the icons of tomorrow. The Nordic design scene today has the will and ability to create something new, and there are many people who are putting some exciting new designs out there – long-lasting designs that definitely have the potential to push Danish and Nordic design into a new era. The traditions are not abandoned, but form the basis of new ideas. So when I think of Nordic design today, I think of it as strong, daring and promising.

ABOVE 'Hello' floor lamp, by Jonas Wagell

OPPOSITE 'Knot' chair, by Tatsuo Kuroda

NORM ARCHITECTS

Jonas Bjerre-Poulsen and co-owner Kasper Rønn instinctively know how to create inspiring environments in which to showcase Nordic cuisine, and have received many awards including the Red Dot Online Award and IF Design Award. Both have backgrounds in design, having worked for Elle Decor, Kinfolk, Dwell and Vogue magazines, as well as creating products for Georg Jensen and Royal Copenhagen.

OPPOSITE 'Norm Dinnerware', 2011, for Höst

WHY DID YOU SET UP NORM ARCHITECTS?

We had worked together at Ole Palsby's studio for over five years, before deciding to establish our own studio, based on our shared tastes and understanding of design, although with very different but complementary approaches to design and architecture. We have worked together for the last fifteen years in many different workplaces, doing things other than design and architecture. While I focus on aesthetics, materials and theory, Kasper is more interested in shape, technology, inventions and new production methods.

We constantly push each other's ideas and performances, and, as a result, our designs move forward further than if we were working alone. We feel that our two approaches are what create the cohesion. The name 'Norm' was chosen because it was important for us to work with traditions and norms that have existed and been refined through millennia, instead of always searching for something new.

DO YOU HAVE A PROCESS THAT YOU WORK THROUGH WHEN DESIGNING?

Our inspirations and processes are extremely diverse. We don't have a special way of working, or a formula for gathering inspiration. Sometimes we see an old product and think to ourselves that it's great, but with a new technology we could improve its look or function. A manufacturing process, a visit to a factory or a talk with a craftsman, or certain shapes in graphics or ideas in a piece of art inspire us. Occasionally, we analyse everyday situations rationally to uncover needs that are not yet fulfilled by other products in the market. Sometimes an idea just starts out with the fascination of a material or surface; sometimes we get a precise brief from a producer. But what we think makes us different from many other designers is that we almost never work with our hands – making models, and so on. We don't have any hands-on experience with crafts, and instead bring the analytical approach of architects.

DO YOU COLLABORATE WITH ANY OTHER DESIGNERS?

We collaborate with Menu as art directors, and have curated a furniture and lighting collection for them, featuring some of the most talented designers in the world. We also designed and launched a range of outdoor furniture for Design Within Reach, based in the US.

HOW DOES DANISH DESIGN DIFFER FROM THAT OF OTHER COUNTRIES?

Danish design has a strong focus on interiors, because we spend so many hours inside owing to the somewhat harsh weather, and on the need to bring the outdoors in – both in the way we use natural light and in the materials we choose. We often design light, bright and white interiors because of their ability to enlarge the space visually. Big windows also serve as a neutral canvas for natural daylight and allow the play of shadows on the walls. White is an optimal colour for interiors: white surfaces reflect the light and give a feeling of calm – important in optimizing quality of life in a country where the sun is often hidden behind grey clouds. It not only enlarges the space, but also provides a beautiful background for furniture and paintings and, most importantly, takes the focus away from the interior design and concentrates it instead on the life being lived within the house. White to us is something clean, bright, soft, smooth, natural and beautiful – which is why it is so often used in churches, galleries and other spaces where the focus is on what is happening in the building, and not on the building in itself.

WHAT DOES NORDIC DESIGN TODAY REPRESENT TO YOU?

We think that Scandinavian design has always held a strong position globally, but there is no doubt that the strong focus on 'New Nordic' in the culinary world has helped spotlight what is happening in architecture, design and art. In Scandinavia, everything from houses and benches to public restrooms and lamp posts are designed with form and function in mind, and growing up in the midst of it gives us a distinct design advantage. In sympathy with the Scandinavian tradition of simplicity, we strive to cut down to the bone in our designs, finding the simplest shape for a given task without forgetting the beauty of the shape and the details, in order to reach a point where there is nothing to add or take away to make the product better. Scandinavian design is rooted in a sincere devotion to craft, using good materials and creating designs that last. Products should not only be durable because of good craftsmanship, but also durable in the sense that you can keep finding them interesting and beautiful as the years roll by. We take pride in our culture and history, and we hope and aspire to create new norms for Nordic design.

OAXEN KROG

Apart from receiving a Michelin star, Oaxen Krog restaurant also boasts a curious interior inspired by the period from the 1920s to the 1950s, designed by owners Magnus Ek and Agneta Green. The couple collaborated with local artisans and followed their instinct at auctions to create a unique dining experience.

ABOVE A view of the restaurant
OPPOSITE Interior of the Slip

WHAT IS THE BACKGROUND OF YOUR RESTAURANT?

In 1994 we took over a small seasonal restaurant with a fairly simple menu, located in the Stockholm archipelago. We began experimenting with local ingredients and wine pairings to create food experiences. Word spread, and people started coming from all over the world. The restaurant received many awards, and was listed as one of *Restaurant* magazine's 50 Best Restaurants several times. But running a seasonal restaurant on a remote island is difficult, and after seventeen years we moved to Djurgården in Stockholm where we opened the new Oaxen Krog, followed by Slip, a Nordic bistro, in 2013. Djurgården is an oasis in the city: central but close to the outdoors, an

important idea that permeates all our thinking. Now that we're located only ten minutes from downtown Stockholm, it is possible for us to be open all year round.

WHERE DO YOU FIND INSPIRATION FOR YOUR INTERIORS?

We took our inspiration from places such as Hotel New York in Rotterdam and the Riding House Café in London. I have always been interested in mid-century style, and I attended auctions and searched online vintage stores without having a fixed idea of the end result. I would go on instinct, and I would know when I saw something I liked and where it would fit in. The result is an eclectic mix of antique furniture and lighting. We wanted

it to feel as if there had been a restaurant here from the start. One of the nicest compliments I received was from the guest who thought we had been here for thirty years!

WHICH DESIGNERS AND PRODUCERS DID YOU WORK WITH?

We worked with architects Mats Fahlander and Agneta Pettersson for the overall design of the building, but we did most of the interior design ourselves. We used glass from the Orrefors glassworks, but apart from that we relied on antiques or specially commissioned items, including tables by carpenter Johan Linhult and tableware by his wife Sunna Jonsdotter, a potter. Erika Pekkari designed the cushions for the vintage 'Florida' chairs from the Bröderna Wigell factory, and Tärnsjö Garveri produced the leather used to cover the bar, tabletops and the doors between the Slip and Oaxen Krog. I like leather, because it creates a warm atmosphere and ages beautifully.

YOU SEEM TO USE A LOT OF SWEDISH DESIGN. WHY?

We didn't choose Swedish design just for the sake of it, but bought what we enjoy. Much comes from Scandinavia, but the long rows of folding chairs at two of the communal tables in the Slip come from a theatre in London. The tables themselves were found at an antiques fair in Stockholm. They had been used at a school and were a little too low, so we had our carpenter lengthen the legs. It has been quite a lot of work to get all of the details right. I wanted Gense's classic cutlery design 'Tebe' for the Slip, and probably contacted about forty different sellers before I got together the five thousand pieces I needed. The serving plates were found at a flea market, and the flower vases are by my favourite designer, Carl Harry Stålhane.

DO YOU HAVE ANY FAVOURITE PLACES IN SCANDINAVIA THAT INSPIRE YOU?

Rosendals Trädgård, also on Djurgården, is an outdoor café and bakery with a beautiful garden in which they grow their own fruit and vegetables. Everything they serve is organically grown, and

the surroundings are fantastic. It is hard to believe that you are so close to a big city. And, of course, Restaurant AG for the industrial environment and their Porterhouse steaks, and because the owner Johan Jureskog is a dear friend of ours. It is the best place to go in Stockholm if you like beef – the quality is incredible and they will tell you where it comes from, and often even the name of the animal. I recently dined at the famous restaurant Fäviken Magasinet, near Åre, and on the way back, we stopped at the lovely café Jazzköket in Östersund – I would recommend both to anyone visiting the north of Sweden.

WHAT DOES NORDIC DESIGN TODAY REPRESENT TO YOU?

The concept of sustainability permeates everything we do, so we choose to source everything from as nearby as possible. The furniture is, with few exceptions, vintage, from the time when the Swedish furniture industry flourished. In recent years, craftsmanship and expertise had disappeared, but today the interest in quality of design, craft and materials is on the rise again, which is promising. Sustainability applies even more to what we serve. We choose small producers who share our philosophies, and the wellbeing of the animals is of paramount importance. Beverages and ingredients come from Djurgården, the Nordic countries, or – at the very farthest – Europe.

OPPOSITE, ABOVE The interior of the restaurant

OPPOSITE, BELOW A basket of scallops on the deck outside

OBJECTHOOD

Objecthood was set up in 2010 when industrial designer Sofia Ohlsson joined forces with architect Charlotte Elsner and product designer Britta Teleman. Based in Sweden, the trio have won several awards, including the Elle Decoration Swedish Design Award and Svensk Form, and an honourable mention from the City of Stockholm.

HOW DID YOU START OUT?

We began as a loosely connected group of three designers, who slowly grew tighter and transformed into a design studio. Initially, we worked on separate projects and gave each other feedback and help with connections, a type of network that we lacked in Sweden's design community. We didn't know each other, really. I had met Britta in Amsterdam on internships, and Charlotte and Britta met at a lecture in Stockholm. What brought us together was the wish to work in a bigger context. We began to collect our work in a common portfolio, acting as agents for each other to create more opportunities. As we come from different design fields, we complement each other well. It proved to be a winning concept. It is hard work, of course, but working together makes us stronger. We have more to offer our clients, as our skills range from industrial design to architecture. The energy in the group never runs out.

WHERE DO YOU FIND INSPIRATION WHEN YOU BEGIN A NEW DESIGN?

Passionate people. Everyday obstacles. Materials. But we are more driven by human behaviour and the desire to bring joy to the user. As designers, we see it as our mission to add beauty and function to the world. At the same time, we need to compensate for the paradoxical situation in which we want to save the world and still make new products. That is why it is of great importance that our designs last. We try to avoid trends.

IS SWEDISH DESIGN DIFFERENT TO THAT OF OTHER COUNTRIES?

We are not certain it does differ inside the design studios. But when it is filtered through furniture companies and comes out on the market, the designs are marked by how these companies work. The Swedish heritage of wood is ever-present. It has always been accessible and everyone loves it. Sweden still has many small-to-medium furniture companies that produce wood, metal, and more, but the luxury of having factories is something we know we cannot take for granted. Luckily, many producers feel strongly about the need to keep them, and can see the value of keeping them going for as long as possible.

ARE THERE ANY PRODUCERS YOU ARE ESPECIALLY PROUD TO HAVE WORKED WITH?

We don't like looking back, but to have worked with brass producer Skultuna – a Swedish company, founded in 1607 – for a second time is a good thing. We are also proud to have received an honourable mention from the City of Stockholm for our 'Gold Nugget' mobile pavilion.

DO YOU HAVE ANY FAVOURITE PLACES IN SWEDEN THAT INSPIRE YOU?

Småland, the heart of Swedish furniture production, a gigantic forest with a web of tiny villages and an energy that you can feel.

IS THERE ANYTHING THAT AN OUTSIDER SHOULD KNOW ABOUT THE NEW NORDIC DESIGN?

It's all about confidence in terms of visual expression, and honesty in materials and production. A serious take on sustainability is almost taken for granted here.

LEFT 'Pond' table, 2012, for Skandiform

CAROLINE OLSSON

This bright star on the Norwegian product-design scene has already won awards including the Muuto Talent Award, Elle Decoration Norway Young Designer of The Year, and Best Product at 100% Design in London. She likes to gather ideas while trawling through a Swedish flea market, and her designs were included as part of the celebrations for the Hans J. Wegner centenary in Denmark.

WHAT IS YOUR DESIGN PROCESS?

I love to work directly with the material, shaping the object. This is how I would love to work, but because of the limitations of time and access to a workshop, I often start the process with an idea that I draw by hand and then with digital 3D programs. I will usually make mock-ups in paper and other easily available materials to test and adjust the shape, size and functions.

IS DESIGNING IN NORWAY DIFFERENT FROM DESIGNING ANYWHERE ELSE?

One difference is that we are a small design community. There are only a few of us, but we see the advantage of collaborating and sharing experiences. Unfortunately, there is not much production left in Norway, so the majority of local designers depend on cooperating with foreign manufacturers.

WHERE DO YOU GO TO FOR INSPIRATION, BEFORE CREATING A NEW PRODUCT?

One of my favourite places to spend time is Värmland, Sweden, where my father comes from (I'm half-Swedish, half-Norwegian). I love to spend quiet time in the countryside, swimming in the lake or strolling along a country road. I also love visiting the flea markets (*loppis*, in Swedish).

WHAT HAVE BEEN SOME OF YOUR HIGHLIGHTS AS A DESIGNER?

I founded my own design studio in 2013, during my final year studying product design at Akershus University College, in Oslo. My proudest moment as a designer was being invited to exhibit at the Hans J. Wegner centenary in Denmark in 2014. As well as running my own company, I also work as a project coordinator at the Norwegian Centre for Design and Architecture.

ARE THERE ANY NORWEGIAN OR SCANDINAVIAN DESIGNERS THAT YOU ARE PARTICULARLY INSPIRED BY?

All of my colleagues at Klubben, the Norwegian Designers Union, an initiative founded by designers with backgrounds in furniture and product design. There is a boom in young, talented designers from Norway right now. Well-established design groups such as StokkeAustad, Permafrost, Anderssen & Voll and Andreas Engesvik have opened up new doors for the next generation.

LEFT 'Skog' lamps, manufactured by Magnor Glassverk

TIMO RIPATTI

Helsinki-based architect, interior and furniture designer Timo Ripatti runs his own design studio, as well as teaching at Aalto University and the Institute of Design, Lahti University of Applied Sciences. He won Furniture Designer of the Year in Finland, and has shown his designs at the Stockholm Furniture Fair and the Eco-Design exhibition during the Salone del Mobile.

TELL ME ABOUT YOURSELF AS A DESIGNER.

I work as an independent designer and was awarded Furniture Designer of the Year 2010 in Finland. In addition to my design work, I teach furniture design at Aalto University and at Lahti University of Applied Sciences. I set up Studio Ripatti in 2003, after working for architectural firms as an interior architect on large-scale projects. The studio is located in a lively, cooperative space, with several other small studios, including graphic, textile and product designers, architects, a photographer and artists.

WHERE DO YOU FIND INSPIRATION?

My sources of inspiration vary, but some I return to regularly. Art in all its different forms is a significant source of inspiration; the same goes for architecture. Being in the outdoors (such a cliché!) gives me peace, tranquillity and a feeling of relaxation, more so than direct shapes or concepts. When travelling, I always visit local

art exhibitions, architectural sites and natural attractions. Seeing something 'wrong' is a very important source of inspiration.

WHAT DOES THE FUTURE HOLD FOR YOUR DESIGN STUDENTS?

There are so many designers graduating today, and in a sense it feels as though there can't be enough work for all of them. But on the other hand, there is design in everything that people do. The designers of tomorrow must seek new ways of working. We must focus on a much broader field of design.

WHAT DOES FINNISH DESIGN MEAN TO YOU?

The golden era of Finnish design springs from a historically rural society's need for highly functional yet affordable everyday objects, and from the post-war shortage of both materials and money. In the 1950s Finnish design was acknowledged internationally as democratic, super-functional and affordable. Nowadays, I don't think it differs very much from the globally accepted 'common western' style. Design is not a nationality-driven thing. It's an 'added value'-driven business, regardless of where the designer or the company comes from.

WHAT PLACES IN SCANDINAVIA INSPIRE YOUR WORK AS A DESIGNER?

Trekking in the mountainous areas of northern Finland, Sweden or Norway, and kayaking or sailing on the Baltic Sea. A dream place to visit one day is Iceland, which might not – strictly speaking

– be part of Scandinavia, but is part of the Nordic heritage. Cities that are particularly nice to visit are Helsinki, Stockholm, Oslo and Copenhagen.

HOW DO THE NORDIC COUNTRIES DIFFER FROM EACH OTHER IN TERMS OF DESIGN?

There are excellent designers and companies in Sweden and Denmark. There are also very good designers in Finland and Norway, but sadly a smaller number of great companies. Nordic design continues to be excellent, even if it's not so typically 'Nordic' any more. Contemporary Nordic designers are taking design into the future in a great way.

OPPOSITE 'Kuppi' lights, 2013

BELOW 'Säle' table, 2013

EVA SCHILDT

Eva Schildt has worked for Japanese companies Askul and Uniqlo, as well as Swedish giants Ikea and Svenskt Tenn. In 2011 she formed her own design studio, and her 'Grace 3' credenza was shown at the London Design Festival 2013. She has also created a range of vases for Swedish firm Klong.

WHERE DID YOU WORK BEFORE SETTING UP YOUR OWN COMPANY?

After graduating from Beckmans College of Design, I worked for several Swedish companies, including Design House Stockholm, Svenskt Tenn (p. 26), Ikea, Playsam and Klong. I also spent a couple of years in Japan, working for Askul, Actus, Cibone and Uniqlo. Recently, I developed a range of storage furniture for Skandium (p. 246).

WHAT ARE YOUR THOUGHTS ABOUT DESIGN?

I always try to be observant and to notice things that appeal to me, or are smart or clever in some way. The key is to remember them and put them together in a new way. You have to be honest in your intentions regarding a design, and in its function and production.

WHAT IS THE FOCUS OF SWEDISH DESIGN?

Simplicity and functionality, and natural materials. Colours are often light or bluish-cool. Nordic design today means design that works in everyday life and for all people. I like to think of it as inclusive.

ABOVE 'Äng' vase, 2013, for Klong

OPPOSITE 'Gardener's Sofa', 2011, for Design House Stockholm

WHAT HAS BEEN YOUR MOST SUCCESSFUL DESIGN TO DATE?

My bestselling item is the 'Äng' vase for Klong. But as far as design experiences go, I think working in Japan and learning about another culture and their design traditions was valuable.

DO YOU HAVE ANY FAVOURITE PLACES IN SCANDINAVIA THAT INSPIRE YOU?

The island of Gotland has an extraordinary landscape and beauty all year round. A visit to the Louisiana Museum of Modern Art always gives me energy and provides inspiration. I think the mix of the old house and modern extension, the fantastic view and the garden create a universe in itself.

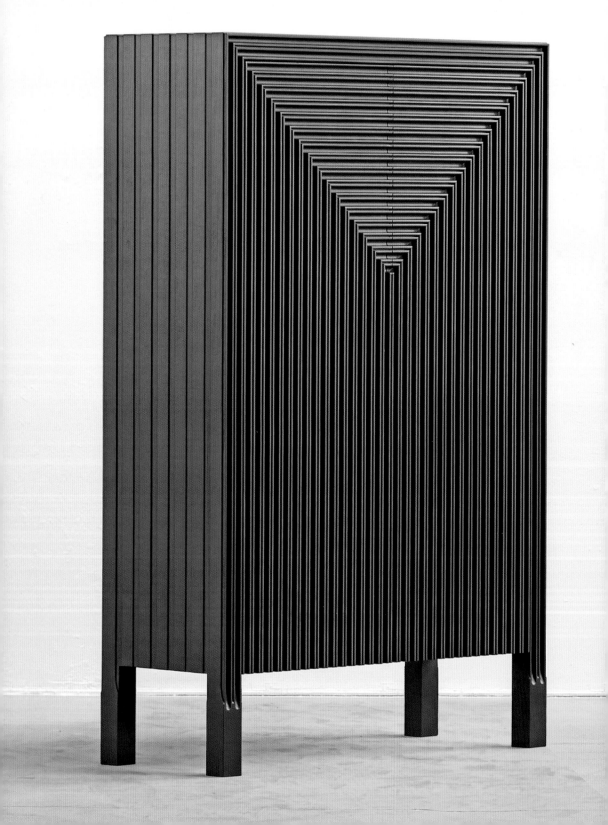

SNICKERIET

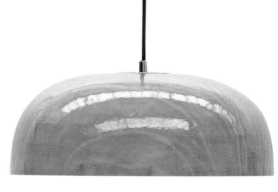

Based in Stockholm, Snickeriet was co-founded by Karl-Johan Hjerling to combine design with fine craftsmanship. Its furniture designs have received numerous awards and been featured in magazines including Wallpaper and Monocle. The firm has also created retail spaces for Swedish clothing brand Acne Studios.

ABOVE 'Få' pendant light, by Karl-Johan Hjerling and Karin Wallenbeck

OPPOSITE 'Korint' cabinet, 2014, by Karl-Johan Hjerling

WHAT IS THE BACKGROUND OF YOUR COMPANY?

Snickeriet was founded in 2012 by a group of like-minded cabinet-makers and designers. We wanted to combine the design and manufacture of our own furniture line with bespoke interior projects. We work in small scale and with personal involvement.

WHAT ARE YOUR KEY INSPIRATIONS?

The process of creation is organic and infinitely complex. Our products – when complete – should function as artefacts and speak of a certain purity.

HOW DOES SWEDISH DESIGN DIFFER FROM THAT OF OTHER COUNTRIES?

Nationality is not a very important consideration in our designs, but it is possible that others viewing our work from afar are more conscious of it than we are. We do enjoy exploring the possibilities of local materials, however.

WHAT HAS BEEN YOUR GREATEST ACHIEVEMENT SO FAR?

Continuing to work together and realizing our visions with integrity – ideally to the benefit of others – is all we can ask for.

WHAT ARE YOUR FAVOURITE PLACES IN SCANDINAVIA FOR INSPIRATION?

We like the soon-to-be demolished area of Slussen in Stockholm, and the outer archipelago in Gothenburg.

WHAT DOES NORDIC DESIGN MEAN TO YOU TODAY?

We welcome the more pluralist and undefined cultural mix that is developing in Scandinavia now, with all the possibilities that this brings for individual expression.

MARTIN SOLEM

Norwegian designer Martin Solem is based in Copenhagen, and also works for design studio Hay. While at the well-known Danish firm Rud Rasmussen earlier in his career, he produced classic furniture designs by Kaare Klint and Børge Mogensen, among others. Solem's own designs have been shown in Paris, London, Stockholm and Oslo.

YOUR DESIGNS ARE A MIX OF BOTH NORWAY AND DENMARK. WHY?

When I turned twenty, I decided to move from Norway to Copenhagen to learn more about Danish furniture and its history. For the next six months I worked at Rud Rasmussen, one of the oldest Danish carpentry companies, which is still producing. I was lucky to work on old classics by designers such as Kaare Klint, Børge Mogensen and Mogens Koch. I also gained a Master's degree from the Royal Danish Academy of Fine Arts, and am currently working on my own projects, as well as working full-time at Hay (p. 120).

THESE PAGES 'Wooden Profile', graduation project, Royal Danish School of Design

ARE ANY OF YOUR DESIGNS INSPIRED BY YOUR NORWEGIAN BACKGROUND?

I think that experiencing the natural world during my childhood in Norway – growing up along the coast and spending holidays in the mountains – has played a big role in shaping who I have become. I think who you are has a huge influence on what you are inspired by as a designer. I like to use observations from everyday life. Ideas can spring from certain shapes or functions, which are usually far from the final product. Unfortunately, I forget a lot of my observations. I always end up with a more thoughtful version of my first impressions.

WHAT DO YOU BELIEVE THE FUTURE HOLDS FOR NORWEGIAN DESIGN?

I think Norwegian design will play a bigger role in Scandinavian design than ever before. It might even play a key role. What inspires me today are all the young, talented Scandinavian designers, who will build on the region's unique design history.

SPACE COPENHAGEN

Design studio Space Copenhagen
was established in 2005 by Signe
Bindslev Henriksen and Peter
Bundgaard Rützou, graduates
of the Royal Danish Academy
of Fine Arts. Together they
have designed interiors for some
of the world's most influential
restaurants including Noma,
Geranium and Geist, along
with products for Georg Jensen,
Fredericia Furniture and Mater.

WHAT IS THE BACKGROUND OF YOUR COMPANY?

We have known each other for a long time, and
have had the studio together for the last ten years.
We share a love for the small-scale, in terms of both
space and details, and an interest in projects where
we can control the spatial, structural and finishing
aspects. We work on everything from interior design
to furniture and objects for everyday use, as well as
artistic installations and art direction.

WHAT ARE THE PRINCIPLES BEHIND SPACE COPENHAGEN?

We believe that design should attempt to
understand the human condition, the defining
rituals and sensibilities involved in each
circumstance, whether a spatial relationship (like
a restaurant) or a more tangible piece of design
(such as a chair). When deciding how to approach
a design, we try not to let ourselves be restricted
by a set notion or reference. Inspiration may be
anything with a sensory coherency, a space, a
conversation, a movement, a sound or a work of
literature, historical motifs, places of coincidence.
We are endlessly fascinated by art, culture, nature
and sensations – anything that relates in context.

ABOVE Restaurant Kul, Copenhagen, 2014

OPPOSITE Dinesen Flooring showroom,
Copenhagen, 2009

WHO ARE YOUR MAIN CLIENTS?

We have many different clients with different backgrounds and profiles. Chefs, hotels, private individuals, furniture manufacturers, fashion and jewelry brands, and so on.

WHAT HAS BEEN YOUR GREATEST ACHIEVEMENT SO FAR?

We enjoy the process more than any specific achievement. It has been wonderful to embrace diverse assignments and challenges, engaging with the specific details of a project or location, as well as with the ambitions and talents of the people involved.

HOW DO YOU SEE NORDIC DESIGN'S IMPACT ON THE GLOBAL SCENE?

In an international context, the Nordic countries might be small, but it still feels like a privilege to be born here. There is something special about it. It might be being part of a well-structured society with high social standards, or the close relationship between the city and the outdoors – a certain slowness and smallness of scale. It is a good place to think. We enjoy our hometown of Copenhagen, which seems to be evolving in a number of directions, and has a certain energy in terms of art, food, music and culture. We have been fortunate to be a part of it, and to work with a lot of talented people. The feedback makes you strive and dream.

WHAT IS IT LIKE TO BE PART OF A NEW GENERATION OF NORDIC DESIGNERS?

The legacy of a heritage with such strong, iconic designs has been somewhat of an obstacle to moving on. But Nordic design is not about exact expression, shape or form. The aesthetics associated with it originate from a mindset indigenous to Scandinavia or northern Europe. For a while, Nordic design was tied to icons such as Arne Jacobsen's 'Egg' chair or Hans J. Wegner's 'Wishbone' chair, as well as a fixed set of textures, from soap-finished oak to leather in light colours. Many designers and manufacturers have found it difficult to emerge from its long shadow. But the real reason why Nordic design achieved world recognition perhaps lies in the motivation process. Scandinavian society consists of fairly small populations within a well-organized social system, in which most people have access to education and freedom of choice. It is also a part of the world that historically, owing to rough weather conditions and a scarce supply of natural resources, thinks and acts according to a set of almost aesthetic values. Scandinavians have an openness, a curiosity and an appetite for travel and culture. We observe, consider and filter those observations, and put them in a new context. This mindset is, in our opinion, the essence of the new Nordic design. It feels as though we are stepping out of the shadows, and the wheels are turning once again.

SPARK DESIGN SPACE

Reykjavik-based Spark was set up by Sigríður Sigurjónsdóttir, a former professor of product design at the Iceland Academy of the Arts. After seeing so many good prototypes go to waste, he decided to create a gallery that would support up-and-coming product designers, and see their work all the way through the production process.

OPPOSITE Storage by Sigríður Sigurjónsdóttir and Snæfríð Thorsteins

WHAT DO YOU THINK YOUR UPBRINGING IN ICELAND HAS GIVEN YOU?

I had a very comfortable upbringing in Garðabær, a suburb of Reykjavik. Now it seems a middle-class, homogeneous neighbourhood, but as a child it was a wonderful place to play in and explore, close to the sea and full of building sites. I never saw it as boring until I grew older. When I think back, I am sure that this safe environment with my mother at home gave me courage. I think that if I had a more difficult or challenging upbringing, I might have chosen a safer path.

WHAT IS YOUR DESIGN BACKGROUND?

For the past four years I have run Spark Design Space, the only design galley in Reykjavik. It is a platform for design projects with a focus on local initiatives involving collaborations between designers and other professions. Each exhibition lasts for about three months. Afterwards, we stock the display pieces in our shop, and are very slowly building up a stock of work we love. I founded Spark when I was still a professor at the Iceland

Academy of the Arts. During my time there, I came across many interesting projects that never went further than the prototype stage. Of course, this is the nature of student work, but I found it frustrating to see all these great designs go to waste. So Spark is about spotting potential and taking it further, all the way to the consumer. Before joining the academy in 2004, I carried out research on new technology and personal space at Central Saint Martins in London, and worked in the fields of new technology and cultural localization both there and in Amsterdam. While at the academy, I initiated a research project called Designers and Farmers, with the aim of developing produce of the highest quality. Design and traceability are key. The project's novelty lay in the bringing together of one of the oldest professions in the country (farming) and one of the newest (product design).

WHAT IS IT LIKE DESIGNING IN SUCH A REMOTE PLACE?

There is a feeling of freedom, as well as isolation. These are contrasting phenomenons, but together

they seem to foster good conditions for creativity.
The lack of both materials and a production
industry has resulted in unique projects, and
designers have found themselves working with,
for example, a net-making factory (Austurland:
Designs From Nowhere) and the fish industry
(Something Fishy). For the latter, Brynjar
Sigurðarson borrowed a 'new' craft from fishermen,
which he applied to his 'Sticks' design. All of these
projects are represented by Spark Design Space.

WHAT DO YOU BELIEVE THE INFLUENCES ARE ON ICELANDIC PRODUCT DESIGN?

Product design in Iceland is very much influenced
by the limitations I mentioned earlier, and by
finding opportunities within these limitations.
Icelandic design has increasingly become a
conversation between different professions.
It follows trends that are happening in the rest of
the world, such as an emphasis on local materials
and the environment. For some reason, Icelandic
design is very colourful at the moment, with a tribal
element that I have not seen before: 'arctic tribal'.

WHAT ARE YOUR OWN DESIGNS INSPIRED BY?

I was originally inspired by the opportunities
in front of me at the Iceland Academy of the
Arts. The 'Bongo Blíða' series was inspired by
the devaluation of the krona and my fear that
I would never be able to travel again. 'Shelve Life',
designed with Snæfríð Thorsteins, was inspired by
the fact that we both constantly lose our keys.
I also seek inspiration from the people around me.
A good conversation can spark an idea. It can also
solve problems, or make things more complicated
and interesting. If I am working on something and
get stuck, it usually works to go for a walk or a
ride on my horse. It clears my head.

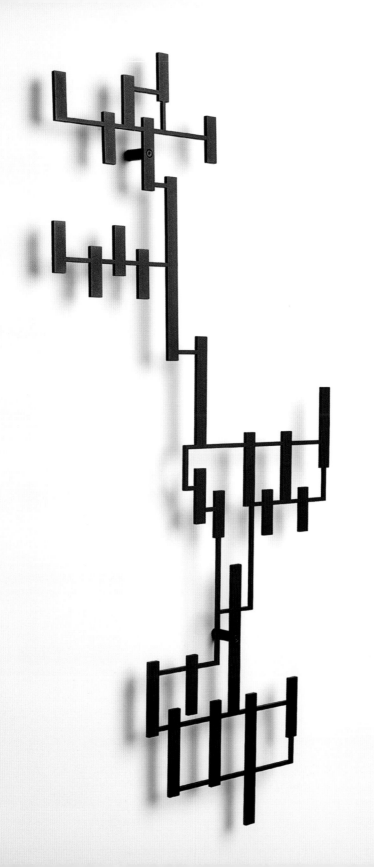

STUDIO FEM

Founded by Anders Engholm Kristensen, Sarah Cramer and Britt Rasmussen, Studio Fem's furniture designs have won numerous awards, including the Hay Talent Award 2014 – even though their designs are still at the prototype stage.

WHAT IS THE BACKGROUND OF YOUR COMPANY?

Studio Fem is based on the idea of synergy. We are three very different designers, and find that it is the interactions between us when we are designing that give us the best results. Our philosophy is that design should be both seen and experienced. The balancing act between functionality and aesthetics is our main focus. Our passion is to design products that push boundaries and arouse curiosity.

HOW DOES DANISH DESIGN DIFFER FROM THAT OF OTHER COUNTRIES?

Because of the globalized world we live in, the simple aesthetics that characterize Danish design are seen in products made by designers from all over the world. We think what distinguishes Danish design from other countries, including other Nordic countries, is our heritage. Denmark is very much a design nation: we were brought up surrounded by architecture and design from the 1950s – the golden age of Danish design. The designers from that era combined their ideas of democratic and modernist design with great craftsmanship, and made Danish design a brand. Today we have other opportunities when it comes to manufacturing, but the aesthetics remain very much the same.

ABOVE 'Buglife' set of tables

OPPOSITE, ABOVE 'Waffle' bench

OPPOSITE, BELOW 'Waffle' sideboard

DO YOU WORK WITH ANY FURNITURE COMPANIES?

All of our designs are still at the prototype stage, but we do work with various firms, including Andersen Furniture and OneCollection – companies that have acted as our mentors and have been a big support from the beginning. Hopefully, our collaborations will result in some great designs in the near future.

WHAT HAS BEEN YOUR GREATEST ACHIEVEMENT SO FAR?

Seeing how well people around the world have reacted to our designs, and being recognized for our work, especially at furniture fairs in Milan and London. And, of course, our success in the Hay Talent Awards 2014 and participation in the Pure Talents Contest, at IMM Cologne 2015.

DO YOU HAVE ANY FAVOURITE PLACES IN SCANDINAVIA THAT INSPIRE YOU?

Stockholm and Copenhagen are both great cities for inspiration, but one of the greatest inspirations Scandinavia has to offer is the outdoors, especially in the northern part of the region. Our all-time favourite place is a lighthouse located at the easternmost part of Jutland, in Denmark. We often come here when we are starting new projects and need to work over the weekend.

THESE PAGES 'Bendy' bench

THE APARTMENT

Danish interior designer
Tina Seidenfaden Busck
transformed an eighteenth-
century apartment in
Copenhagen into a glamorous,
creative space with furniture
by leading Swedish and Finnish
designers. Although it looks
like a private home, everything –
from the chandeliers to
the carpets – is for sale.

HOW DID THE APARTMENT COME ABOUT?

It began with a desire to create a space where I could showcase my own curated selection of vintage pieces and works by contemporary designers that I admire. The Danish interior-design scene is, with good reason, very much influenced by our heritage: sleek forms, functional designs and subdued colours. I wanted to exhibit a more colourful palette than is usually seen in Denmark, introducing Italian mid-century design and contemporary designers from around the globe. When this apartment became available, it all made sense: I designed the space to look like a private home, where everything can be taken home, from the art on the walls to the furniture and lighting. Everything is for sale, and we change the interiors on a regular basis.

WITH YOUR BACKGROUND IN MODERN DESIGN, WHY CHOOSE A PERIOD SPACE?

My aesthetic is very much rooted in a mix of different styles and eras. To me, art and design become more interesting when they get a bit of 'resistance' from other objects that are not necessarily similar. I love the way the Hammershøi-like rooms, with their wood panelling and oak floors, take on a new life through the changing backdrops of contemporary art, mid-century designs, vintage rugs and beautiful lighting.

WHERE DOES YOUR INTEREST IN INTERIORS COME FROM?

You could say I gained an interest in art and design at an early age. I grew up in a creative environment: my father was an art collector, and he always took me to auction houses and galleries. Later on, I went to work for Sotheby's, where I was lucky enough to be immersed in the world of modern art, design and decorative arts, and to gain an in-depth knowledge of the art market.

IS THE DESIGN AN INTENTIONAL MIX OF NORDIC DESIGN AND CONTEMPORARY LIVING?

I have always had a deep interest in interior design, with a very playful and perhaps not very Nordic approach. When I created The Apartment,

I wasn't looking to make a particularly Nordic concept, but I did want to shine a light on Swedish and Finnish designers. Denmark has excellent galleries, such as Dansk Møbelkunst and Klassik, but for some reason iconic Swedish and Finnish designers such as Josef Frank and Alvar Aalto (see Artek; p. 20) have not been very visible on the Danish interior-design scene. I particularly love the beautiful, colourful designs that Frank created for Svenskt Tenn (p. 26) during the 1930s and '40s. We also showcase Danish modern pieces, such as Børge Mogensen's wicker coffee table and Hans J. Wegner's 'PP129' lounge chair in a vibrant red lacquer. I find it interesting to place these pieces in a less formal setting than a traditional gallery space. My aim is that The Apartment should look and feel like a place where people can imagine sitting down to dinner or reading a book. This desire has really been fulfilled by Ilse Crawford (p. 252), who transformed the interiors, including the restaurant.

DO YOU HAVE ANY FAVOURITE DESIGNERS, INTERIORS OR PLACES?

In Denmark, I always recommend the Louisiana Museum of Modern Art. It has an exceptional collection of modern and contemporary art, and the buildings and sculpture park are worth a visit in themselves. Since 2008, the private home of Finn Juhl (p. 24), north of Copenhagen, has been open to the public. The house has its original interiors, with Juhl's own sketches, art collection and personal objects. I have stayed at Ett Hem in Stockholm on several occasions. It is impressive to see how Ilse Crawford and her team have succeeded in making it feel like a home; there is a warmth and an atmosphere that I have not experienced elsewhere in a hotel. Wanås in southern Sweden is known for its superb sculpture park, where artists including Louise Bourgeois and Olafur Eliasson (p. 88) have exhibited their work.

WHAT IS BEHIND THE ENDURING POPULARITY OF NORDIC FURNITURE?

I think the reason Nordic design has had such an international appeal since the 1950s has a lot to do with its timeless aesthetic. The fine craftsmanship and the understated, utilitarian beauty has stood up well to changing fashions. In my own home and at The Apartment, Danish design pieces add character and atmosphere – and being Danish myself, they also add a comforting feeling of history.

WHO ARE THE FUTURE STARS OF NORDIC DESIGN?

Signe Bindslev Henriksen and Peter Bundgaard Rützou of Space Copenhagen (p. 194); they redesigned Noma in 2011. Cecilie Manz (p. 150), because her sculptural designs build on the heritage of Danish Modernism, as well as adding something new and interesting. Rune Bruun Johansen for his simple, elegant designs, which are handmade in Denmark and combine luxurious materials and fine detailing. And Københavns Moebelsnedkeri, one of Scandinavia's most skilled joineries – they made an exquisite built-in wardrobe in smoked oak for The Apartment.

ANNA THÓRUNN

Young Icelandic designer Anna Thórunn combines humorous details with the often harsh environment of her native country. Having studied in Rome and at the Iceland Academy of the Arts, she draws on her experience of both worlds when working in her studio at the collective space Epal.

HOW HAS YOUR ICELANDIC UPBRINGING AFFECTED YOUR DESIGN?

I was brought up in a suburb of Reykjavik, which was full of new residents, and very creative and exciting for a young girl. Our street was surrounded by wild countryside, and today I realize what a privilege it was growing up in such a beautiful and peaceful place. Iceland's folk tales also played a big part in my upbringing. My father was a pilot with Icelandair, and we often travelled with him. These trips to exciting places broadened my horizons. The average Icelander at the time was very influenced by anything to do with the US, and so was I, but today my designs are inspired by other cultures, as well. There was only one national television station back then, and every July the staff would go on holiday, so families had to make their own entertainment, whether visiting relatives or playing outside in the twenty-four-hour daylight.

ABOVE 'Feed Me' bowl
BELOW 'Styrkur' lamp
OPPOSITE 'Kolur 305' lamp

Iceland's harsh elements will affect any youngster brought up there, especially those of us who remember winters that were less mild than they are now. I remember holding on to street lamps to avoid being blown away, and it was not unusual to wade through waist-high snow. The short winter days and long hours of darkness have, without doubt, had the greatest effect on my designs. The nostalgia in my work reflects the experience of losing my father at a very young age and having to grow up fast.

WHAT DID YOU DO BEFORE SETTING UP YOUR STUDIO?

I began my design career while studying at the Istituto Europeo di Design, in Rome. While there, I began to question if I was on the right track, and enrolled in a goldsmithing and jewelry-design course at the Scuola Orafa, before becoming an apprentice to a Roman goldsmith. After six years in Italy, I moved back to Iceland and began studies at the Technical College in Hafnarfjörður, where I graduated in art and design. It was there that I finally found my calling. I graduated with another degree in product design from the Iceland Academy of the Arts in 2007, and have worked as an independent designer ever since.

WHY DID YOU DECIDE TO SET UP YOUR OWN STUDIO?

I decided it would be best to keep true to my nature and work as an independent designer and producer. I work alone, but share a workshop with a few other designers at the Epal design studio in Reykjavik.

DO YOU HAVE ANY FAVOURITE PLACES THAT INSPIRE YOU?

Where I get my inspiration and ideas from varies. It can be from everyday life and activities, or from memories related to my childhood. Usually I keep my ideas to myself and develop them in my head,

before sketching them on paper. To begin with I have a fairly clear idea, but sometimes it takes a while for it to become fully developed. When I need inspiration, I go for a walk along the shore or in the wild Icelandic landscape, and the ideas will come flowing back to me.

WHAT IS IT LIKE TO CREATE MODERN DESIGN IN SUCH A REMOTE PLACE?

I truly believe it is not important where one's home is located. Creativity and design have no borders – the world is a global market without boundaries, and with the technology we have today it is very easy to be influenced by design trends from all over the world. It is, however, important to remain true to yourself. I can't deny that there are some big advantages to designing in such an isolated place. What I like about Iceland is how quickly you can be surrounded by wild countryside, where I can be alone with my thoughts and find the answers to all my questions.

DO YOU HAVE ANY FAVOURITE ICELANDIC DESIGNERS AT THE MOMENT?

From what can be seen over the last few years, Icelandic design is in good health and thriving. Individual designers are making waves with their design, and work all over the world. The fact that Icelandic designers suffer somewhat owing to their location should be expected from any small economy. The designers I find most interesting at the moment are those that graduated with me from the Iceland Academy of the Arts, such as Thórunn Árnadóttir and Unnur Valdís, who designed the 'Float' swimming cap.

ATLE TVEIT

Norwegian furniture designer
Atle Tveit graduated from the
Bergen Academy of Art and
Design, and now works for
various Scandinavian furniture
manufacturers. He has won
several awards, including the
Norwegian Design Council's
Young Talent Award.

OPPOSITE 'Bird' sofa, produced by Helland

**IS DESIGNING IN NORWAY DIFFERENT
FROM DESIGNING IN OTHER COUNTRIES?**

In terms of the design process, I'm not sure it is all
that different. But Norway is a small country, so
there is limited industry compared to, for example,
Germany. The market and customer base is also
much smaller. It seems wise to try and approach the
industry on a global scale, but you can also work in
an interdisciplinary way or within your own niche
to find less competition and more projects.

WHAT IS YOUR BACKGROUND?

I was born in a small place called Nevlunghavn,
on the southeast coast of Norway, but moved
to Bergen to study furniture and interior design.
After graduating in 2006 I set up a design studio
with a fellow graduate, and we soon began getting
commissions and a lot of press interest. We
developed furniture for a handful of Scandinavian
manufacturers and won several awards, before we
both left Bergen. Today I run my own design studio,
working from the old control tower at Fornebu, just
outside Oslo. Some projects are my own work, but
I also collaborate with other designers.

WHERE DO YOU FIND INSPIRATION?

Anything and everything. Human beings, problems
that need solving or improving, the outdoors, great
design and architecture, technology and details only
a designer (nerd) would notice. Not necessarily in
that order.

**DO YOU HAVE ANY FAVOURITE PLACES
IN SCANDINAVIA THAT INSPIRE YOU?**

The outdoors always gets my thoughts drifting.
Although I live in Oslo, I have parks, forests and
beaches just outside my doorstep, both at home and
at my office. A quick stroll to clear the head can
often lead to new and interesting ideas. I regularly
go to art exhibitions and design fairs and events.
After a few days with a broad spectrum of visual
impressions, my head can overload and explode
with new ideas. I spend the next few days scribbling
down small, quick sketches. Some might be worth
looking into, but most won't survive beyond a few
minutes of sketching.

WHAT IS YOUR DESIGN PROCESS LIKE?

It varies, depending on where the ideas come from.

They can spring from a sudden inspiration while I'm on a plane or out hiking, and I will have to take notes or make a few quick sketches. If I'm working on a brief or a commission, I would normally start by identifying the needs of my client (which also means the buyer), analysing the task at hand and considering all the important factors within the project: cost, production, efficiency, environmental concerns, use of materials, ergonomics, distribution, and so on. In both cases I begin by sketching by hand and digitally, as well as working with physical models. It depends a lot on who I'm working with or for, how much research needs to be done, and when we can begin developing the solution at their facilities.

ARE THERE ANY SCANDINAVIAN DESIGNERS THAT YOU ARE INSPIRED BY?

Although we have a modest design heritage in Norway, I have always found that what we do have – classics like the 'Scandia' chair by Hans Brattrud, the 'Dokka' lamp by Birger Dahl and the 'Modell 711' chair by Fredrik A. Kayser – are impressive and inspirational, right up there with other internationally acclaimed icons. I tend to work from the same philosophy: minimalist aesthetics. There is a certain elegance and harmony in the objects, a simplicity – not easy to achieve – which

I think is universally perceived. In terms of more recent examples, Norway Says opened many doors for Norwegian designers, myself included, and there are more and more up-and-coming talents emerging from the design academies in Oslo and Bergen. It must have something to do with me tutoring part-time at the Bergen Academy of Art and Design...

WHAT ARE YOUR THOUGHTS ABOUT THE FUTURE OF NORWEGIAN DESIGN?

It looks bright. It seems we have all eyes on us, but without the pressure of having to look back at a huge design heritage. Most designers understand that you can be stronger if you pull together, working with each other to lift the value of Norwegian design, rather than competing against anyone and everyone. I think perhaps the competition was harder twenty years ago. Today people seem to understand that by exhibiting as a group in London and Milan, we enhance each other's work, rather than risking being invisible if everyone tried to show one or two pieces individually. If we continue on that path, and allow some of the participants to get more publicity and establish their names internationally, I think Norwegian design can build up a strong position that will last for many years to come.

BJØRN VAN DEN BERG

Oslo-based product designer
Bjørn Van den Berg has already
taken part in several exhibitions,
including the Salone del Mobile,
and the Stockholm Furniture
Fair. Having received an MA
from the University of Oslo and
undertaken an internship at
Anderssen & Voll, he is a talent
to watch.

WHAT ARE THE DIFFICULTIES FACING A YOUNG DESIGNER IN NORWAY?

Because Norway has limited local industry, some
designers choose to go abroad to connect with
manufacturers. In recent years, more young
designers have shown their work at exhibitions.
Another reason for the desire to exhibit is that
quite a few designers have begun working together
in group initiatives, including Klubben, Look To
Norway and OsloForm, and these collaborations
appear to have a strong advantage. Norwegian
design strikes a good balance between projects that
are purely conceptual and those with commercial
potential. Lately designers have begun turning to
accessories, possibly because they are often under-
explored in comparison to furniture.

WHAT PATH DID YOU FOLLOW TO GET TO WHERE YOU ARE NOW?

As a child, I drew a lot and collected things.
I've always been connected to objects and their
aesthetics, and find pleasure in creating experiences,
food or an object. I developed this approach
to design while studying product design at the
University of Oslo and Akershus University
College. My education was practice-based, with
the opportunity to create realistic prototypes

ABOVE 'Aura' series of mirrors, 2014

OPPOSITE Table mirror, from the 'Aura' series

through fieldwork approaches in the design community. In 2014 I finished my thesis, 'Presence and Everyday Objects'; the physical products were developed through exhibitions in Stockholm and Milan. After finishing my studies I took part in exhibitions in London and Tokyo.

WHAT MOTIVATES YOU WHEN CREATING YOUR DESIGNS?

I believe in creating some kind of experience through my design. Often I am searching for good experiences that I can recreate in my projects. Many of my ideas occur while travelling, looking at things around me or while drawing. When developing ideas, the process might be conducted on the bus as at the drawing board. I try to be aware of trends and of people's needs.

WHERE DO YOU GO TO FIND INSPIRATION?

Travelling along the west coast of Norway is something I really have enjoyed. From Jæren in the south, and going north, each fjord and valley has its own character and environment. It is very beautiful and energy-boosting with all that fresh air. Otherwise, Oslo is the place I usually get inspired by since I live there. I spend most of my time in the Sagene and Grünerløkka districts of the city. The parks, exhibitions, restaurants and people are all inspiring – everyday moments, where I have a feeling of presence and awareness.

HOW DO YOU GO ABOUT DESIGNING AN OBJECT?

My process depends on the project, although I always spend quite a long time of thinking and drawing while developing the idea. After a while, I feel ready to visualize the idea as close as possible to what I imagined in 3D-modelling and low-cost mock-ups. I try to get the proportions right and adjust shapes. I also evaluate aspects such as colour and surface to get an impression of an idea's potential by going back and forth between the different media. Eventually, I become more aware of how to design the final prototype.

DO YOU HAVE ANY DESIGNERS THAT YOU LOOK TO FOR INSPIRATION?

I like the work of Finnish designers Timo Sarpaneva and Kaj Franck. They created products in the 1950s and '60s that still feel timeless – a method I think is underestimated in the design profession as a sustainable approach. Extending the life of products by creating them to last for generations is something I'm always working towards. Norway Says has also been a great inspiration, and it still is, in terms of how they have managed to establish themselves and create their own identity in their work. It is difficult to imagine how Norwegian furniture design today would have developed without them.

WHAT DOES THE FUTURE OF NORWEGIAN DESIGN HOLD?

Hopefully, more designers will establish their own studios, and I believe that Norwegian designers will continue working together. My vision is that through such collaboration we will see the emergence of a new golden era.

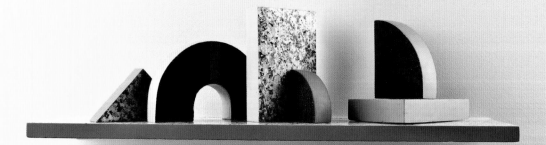

VERA & KYTE

The city of Bergen, on the west coast of Norway, is home to two young designers: Vera Kleppe and Åshild Kyte. The pair work together as interior and furniture designers, and have been cited in Wallpaper, Architectural Digest and Elle Decoration. They were nominated at the Nova Design Awards, and won the Danish Design Award in 2014.

WHY DID YOU CHOOSE BERGEN AS A BASE FOR YOUR COMPANY?

For us, Bergen was a natural choice. It is a small city, with a large and active cultural community. Whether you are an internationally renowned artist or just starting out, there is a strong sense of community and new interdisciplinary collaborations spring up continuously. This was one of the main reasons we decided to base our studio here. The beautiful scenery right outside our studio window is an additional attraction.

HOW DID YOU DISCOVER FURNITURE DESIGN AND EACH OTHER?

An interest in aesthetics and making has always been present for both of us, but took many forms before we discovered furniture design. We met during our studies, where we made our first collaborative projects and discovered that we made a great creative team. From then on we wanted to establish our own studio, and set up Vera & Kyte once we finished our MA degrees from the Bergen Academy of Art and Design in 2012. Today we have a spacious studio, and invite graphic designers, musicians and other creatives to share the space with us and give each other new perspectives.

OPPOSITE, ABOVE
'Whiskey and Water' drinking glasses

OPPOSITE, BELOW
'Staged' series of shelves and blocks

WHAT ELSE INSPIRES YOU?

Always something new. Our eclectic approach to design leaves us open to a wide range of influences. Curiosity is central in our approach to design, and keeps us looking. It's a way of constantly seeking new knowledge. First and foremost we are inspired by areas beyond our design arena, such as everyday objects, heavy industry, film, art and architecture. These experiences will often leave us with an impression we want to build on – whether recreating, interpreting or communicating an element of these experiences in an object.

DO YOU HAVE ANY FAVOURITE PLACES THAT YOU KEEP RETURNING TO?

The busy harbour outside our studio, with its scenic landscape, maritime traffic and artistic inhabitants. There is always something new to see. We enjoy strolling around the neighbourhood, stumbling upon new encounters and possibilities.

WHAT IS YOUR DESIGN PROCESS?

This process is unique for each piece, but there are some stages that we always go through. First, a vision for the project is established. Then the 'wall of inspiration', covered with Post-its, is created. Sketches become scale models, which then grow into full-size mock-ups. Switching between digital 3D-modelling and handcrafted models is the most efficient way of getting a feel for the product. Before the first prototype is created, we invite others to give feedback to refresh our perspective.

OPPOSITE 'Apparel' room divider
BELOW 'Balcony' daybed

DO YOU REFERENCE ANY OTHER NORDIC DESIGNERS IN YOUR WORK?

There are a lot of inspiring designers from Scandinavia, both historic and contemporary. Styles, eras and specific projects, rather than one designer's body of work, more often inspire us. One example of a personal favourite, however, is the Norwegian furniture designer Sven Ivar Dysthe (p. 18), particularly for the collection he designed for the Henie-Onstad Art Centre, which is both striking in its own right and reflects the architecture beautifully.

WHAT DO YOU BELIEVE TO BE THE FUTURE OF NORWEGIAN DESIGN?

Exciting. Expanding. Exploring. We can't wait to be a part of it!

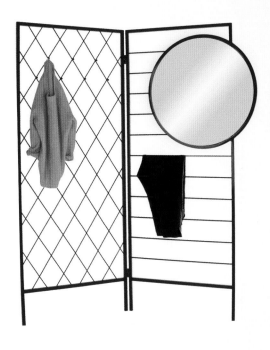

PART 3

INTERNATIONAL
COMMENTATORS

AMANDA DAMERON

Heralded as 'one of the most influential voices in the world of modern design', Amanda Dameron has worked in the fields of architecture and design for over fifteen years. Prior to becoming editor-in-chief at Dwell magazine, she served as editor at Architectural Digest and joined Dwell Media as digital director in 2008. Her work has been published in Condé Nast Traveller, Vogue Living and Elle Decor.

DO YOU HAVE ANY FAVOURITE PLACES IN SCANDINAVIA THAT INSPIRE YOU?

My favourite cities in Scandinavia are Helsinki and Stockholm, where I love to stay at the Hotel Skeppsholmen. The design by architectural firm Claesson Koivisto Rune is so poetic. It's restrained and powerful, which is how I like to define Scandinavian design in general. I love the city because of its design identity, and how easy it is to get around on foot. My must-visit destinations include Svenskt Tenn (p. 26), Carl Malmsten and AB Nordiska Galleriet, all in Stockholm, and I love the kooky Museum of Ethnography.

WHO ARE AMONG THE OUTSTANDING DESIGNERS THAT HAVE INFLUENCED SCANDINAVIAN STYLE?

This is going to be a long list! Kaare Klint, Kaj Franck, Monica Förster, Note Design Studio, Form Us With Love, Alvar Aalto (see Artek; p. 20), &tradition (p. 44), Arne Jacobsen, Front, Hay (p. 120), Jens Quistgaard, Jens Risom, Anderssen & Voll – a mix of established designers and new talents, who are all outstanding.

ARE THERE ANY NEWCOMERS WE SHOULD LOOK OUT FOR?

There is so much great young talent emerging from all over Scandinavia. I would mention designers such as Vera Kleppe and Ashild Kyte (see Vera & Kyte; p. 222), Jonas R. Stokke and Øystein Austad of StokkeAustad, Nick Ross, Simon Key Bertman, Andreas Engesvik, John Astbury (p. 56); Bengt Brummer; Karin Wallenbeck from the WhatsWhat collective; Dögg Guðmundsdóttir; Ditte Hammerstrøm; Line Depping; Lukas Dahlén; Fredrik Färg . . . I could go on and on!

DOMINIQUE BROWNING

Writer and editor Dominique Browning worked for several international magazines, including Newsweek and Esquire, before becoming editor-in-chief of House & Garden. After the magazine folded in 2007, she launched a new career as an author, writing several books on the home, gardening and lifestyle.

HOW DO YOU SEE THE INFLUENCE OF THE GREAT SCANDINAVIAN DESIGNERS ON DESIGN TODAY?

The influence of Scandinavian design has been enormous – and in the US, at least, it is beginning to be recognized and understood. We have loved, and been influenced by, Scandinavian product design for many years now, but architecture is just beginning to be appreciated. I think that's because there haven't been enough great books showing the treasures of Scandinavian design – most of what we see are items of furniture, pottery or jewelry, shown out of the context of the homes for which they were created, and in which they were loved and used. The connecting of indoor and outdoor spaces, the use of new materials and expansive sheets of glass, the creative flair with humble materials such as cinder blocks, and the focus on grids and regular rhythms and patterns of spaces to make calm envelopes for living – all of these are hallmarks of Scandinavian design.

TELL ME ABOUT LIVING WITH SCANDINAVIAN DESIGN. HOW DID YOU FIRST BECOME AWARE OF IT?

I fell in love with Hans J. Wegner, the chair master, many years ago – and my family gathers for dinner around the table in his wishbone chairs. And who can help but fall in love with Nanna Ditzel's charming 'Egg' of 1959, a wicker nest hanging from a branch (or the ceiling) for all of us little birds to curl up in? Alvar Aalto (see Artek; p. 20) was perhaps the first designer many Americans came to identify, but whether or not we knew their names, many of us grew up surrounded by the furniture of such designers as Finn Juhl (p. 24). Because the American middle class expanded so rapidly after the Second World War, and new houses were being built by the thousands in the new suburbs, there was an enormous need and desire for modern, light furniture. Teak was everywhere. Magazines like *House & Garden* did a lot to promote the new Scandinavian design. And let's not forget

Marimekko! I remember seeing the film *Cries and Whispers* (1972) at university, then going to the shop Design Research and buying the same striped, floor-length cotton T-shirt Liv Ullmann wore in the movie. It was the sexiest and smartest thing, I thought – which goes to show what an egghead I was! I still wear these shirts, all the time. I could go on and on: my heart still responds so deeply to these now-classic designs. They have aged beautifully, and look as fresh and provocative and endearing now as they did when they first came out. You can see how they have influenced so many of today's young designers.

WHO OR WHAT HAS BEEN THE BIGGEST INFLUENCE IN YOUR CAREER?

Probably my mother's Moroccan background. She grew up in Casablanca, and when I was little our house was filled with pieces from Morocco – and Scandinavian teak furniture! The contrast was fantastic. I didn't understand anything about it at the time, of course. But the lesson there was, express yourself! Your home should tell the story of who you are, where you've been and what you've loved. So from a design point of view, that's been a huge influence. The other big influence is books: I read as I breathe. And I find that reading, and gazing at pictures, is the most mind-expanding thing to do. Others can keep their drugs; I get high on books. New horizons, new impressions, new colours, new contrasts, new shapes and patterns and proportions: we should all expose ourselves constantly to the provocation of the unfamiliar and unexpected. Even if, afterwards, we return to the good old familiar loves.

HAVE YOU COME ACROSS ANY NEW TALENT FROM SCANDINAVIA?

Let's just say that I could spend all my money at Skandium (p. 246), and all the other places that champion new young designers. The tradition of great, spare, quirky and beautiful design lives on.

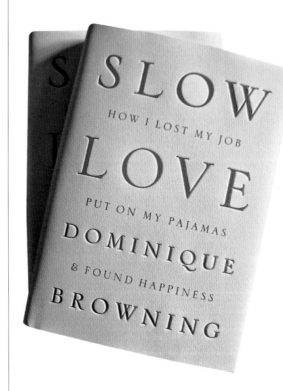

SUSANNA VENTO

Finnish interior designer Susanna Vento is also the writer behind the successful blog Varpunen. She currently works for Deko magazine, and her interior style has been featured in Dwell. Among her many clients are Iittala and Marimekko.

WHAT IS YOUR DEFINITION OF FINNISH DESIGN?

I really believe in the style and expertise of Scandinavian designers when it comes to creating products for a broad public. Design in Finland does not have a very long history, and is focused on demand, while at the same time inspired by the wealthy, luxurious style of Europe. Perhaps that is why Finnish designers create versatile, material-based designs that function well in many homes. I believe this is a good thing. In fact, I prefer that furniture is functional, authentic and created by using natural materials – with a pinch of today's trends and good design.

DO YOU HAVE ANY CURRENT FAVOURITE NORDIC DESIGNERS?

Lately I have been following the Finnish fashion brand Samuji and furniture company Aalto + Aalto (p. 48). I also like the Danish designers Cecilie Manz (p. 150) and Mette Duedahl.

WHAT HAS INFLUENCED YOU MOST IN YOUR CAREER?

I am perhaps inspired by my own minimalistic lifestyle and upbringing in Finland. I buy less, but I choose high-quality, well-designed items, instead of mass-produced ones. This way of thinking is key to the Nordic lifestyle generally, and that's the way I look at the world and the designers. I really like to buy furniture that has been carefully produced and designed through craftsmanship.

WHERE DO YOU RECOMMEND GOING IN FINLAND FOR DESIGN-RELATED EXPERIENCES?

In Finland I'd recommend restaurants like Skiffer (on a small island), Pastor and Putte's Bar and Pizza. The Teurastamo area of Helsinki offers the latest pop-up happenings, and restaurants with original and different interior design.

HAVE YOU COME ACROSS ANY NEW TALENT FROM FINLAND?

I just bought a mirror from the Finnish designer Iina Vuorivirta. I really admire her style and vision.

NORDIC DESIGN

Catherine Lazure-Guinard created the award-winning Canadian blog Nordic Design after a life-changing visit to Denmark. It is now the leading blog in North America about Scandinavian design, interiors, architecture and lifestyle.

WHAT ARE YOUR THOUGHTS ABOUT NORDIC DESIGN?

Scandinavia is one of the hottest design destinations, praised for its innovative, functional and sleek contemporary design. Its countries have produced a long list of legendary designers, who have made an enormous contribution to the aesthetics of our modern world. Nordic designers produce objects that are innovative in form and function – honest, thoughtful and modest designs based on the premise that the region's design heritage and traditions of craftsmanship must be respected. They taught us that clean lines and natural materials never go out of style, and satisfied our growing appetite for simplicity, as well as intelligent, quality products. They are proud promoters of the eco-driven 'buy less, but better' mindset, which we should all adhere to.

DO YOU HAVE ANY FAVOURITE DESIGNERS?

I am a huge fan of Norm Architects (p. 172). They share a desire to celebrate their culture and design history, and a love for details, simple forms, quality materials and a timeless aesthetic. Together they create fantastic interiors and products that represent what Scandinavian design is all about.

I believe they are shaping the new Nordic movement, and there is no doubt that they will leave a major mark in Scandinavia's design history. Andreas Engesvik is at the forefront of Norway's blossoming design scene – and rightfully so. He is creative, and often surprises with his numerous ideas and playful Nordic edge. On my wish list is one of his 'Bunad' blankets, inspired by Norway's cultural heritage and traditional folk costumes. I very much like the timeless elegance of Per Söderberg's 'No Early Birds' collection, as well as the eclectic, chic style of fashion and interior designer Malene Birger (p. 72). Of course, I am an admirer of design legends such as Arne Jacobsen and Hans J. Wegner, two driving forces in the Danish Modern movement. Their many trendsetting (and now iconic) pieces from the mid-twentieth century are still very much in demand.

HOW DID YOU GET INTO NORDIC DESIGN, PRODUCTS AND INTERIORS?

It wasn't until I was in my early twenties that I developed an interest in decoration and design, the main reason being that I didn't like what I had access to at the time. I couldn't relate to any style – until I set foot in Denmark. It was like a whole new world was opening up to me. I felt at home right

INTERNATIONAL COMMENTATORS

away, thinking, 'this is it!' I admired the Nordic lifestyle, design and culture, as I made my way across Scandinavia. I found the style functional, smart, timeless, beautiful and sleek. I started the blog in 2010 as a personal design reference, a way to classify all the beautiful interiors, furniture, lighting and home accessories I discovered. I felt so enthusiastic about Scandinavian design, I wanted to share the joy. I was convinced that more people would enjoy this amazing style, just as I did.

WHERE SHOULD SOMEONE WANTING TO EXPERIENCE SCANDINAVIA FOR THE FIRST TIME GO?

I truly feel at home in Copenhagen. I had the chance to live in this bustling and fascinating city, and I would repeat the experience in a heartbeat. Stroll around the city and you will discover an incredible number of design-focused stores: Hay (p. 120), Vipp, Designer Zoo, Normann Copenhagen (p. 168), Stilleben and Royal Copenhagen, to name a few. My ultimate favourite is Illums Bolighus, a massive design mecca – I can spend hours there! I refuel at the Royal Café next door with 'smushi', a sushi-sized version of the traditional Danish smørrebrød. At night, I like to dine at Relae or Höst, two very stylish establishments known for their creative kitchens and no-nonsense gastronomy. For my next trip, I would stay at the luxurious Nimb Hotel or the trendy Hotel sp34 (p. 126), formerly known as Hotel Fox. In the last few years, Oslo has become a seriously cool design and art destination. Thanks to a much-anticipated programme of regeneration, the neighbourhood of Tjuvholmen, or 'Thief Island', is now a vibrant cultural hub. It is filled with galleries, chic hotels and world-class architecture: the Oslo Opera House, the Astrup Fearnley Museum of Modern Art and a Renzo Piano-designed museum, among others. Edgy boutique hotel The Thief is a stylish base from which to explore the revived waterfront

district. I strongly recommend visiting Iceland. Spectacular landscape aside, what puts it up there on my must-see list is the country's most important design festival: DesignMarch. You will discover a burgeoning creative-design culture that is still somewhat under the radar, and different from what you will see in the rest of Scandinavia. I like to stay at Reykjavik Lights Hotel and 101 Hotel. If you venture outside the capital, book a room at the stunning ION Luxury Adventure Hotel. A visit to the Blue Lagoon is a must, too.

ARE THERE ANY NEW NORDIC TALENTS TO WATCH OUT FOR?

Keep an eye on Christina Liljenberg Halstrøm, a graduate of the Royal Danish Academy of Fine Arts, in Copenhagen. She has a beautiful design aesthetic; her recent elegant, minimalist 'Georg' collection for Skagerak was stunning. I am also a fan of Norwegian designer Lars Beller Fjetland (p. 64), including his ingenious 'Re-turned' birds, made of salvaged pieces of wood. Sustainability, sophistication and longevity are at the core of his design philosophy. Caroline Olsson (p. 182) is another designer to watch out for. With a taste for traditional crafts and techniques, she gives a new twist to her fun and creative designs. Her 'Bambi' table is a good example.

KINFOLK

Creative lifestyle studio Ouur, co-founded by Nathan Williams, produces collections of clothing and homewares, as well as Kinfolk, a magazine that has gained an international following. They are based in Portland, Oregon – with offices in Tokyo – but are heavily inspired by the Nordic lifestyle.

GIVEN THAT OUUR IS A BRAND THAT IS FOCUSED ON LIFESTYLE, WHAT ARE YOUR THOUGHTS ABOUT NORDIC DESIGN?

We appreciate how Nordic designs are generally quite simple yet still manage to communicate a sense of warmth and comfort. We have published stories on the Danish concept of *hygge*, which refers to the cosiness that comes when spending time with close friends and family while enjoying good food, though we have no direct translation in English. It seems as though many Nordic designers are influenced by this traditional appreciation of comfort, and their designs reflect that shared value by helping to create welcoming spaces.

OPPOSITE, TOP An issue of *Kinfolk* magazine

OPPOSITE, BOTTOM The magazine celebrates the welcoming elegance of Nordic design

HOW DOES SCANDINAVIA INSPIRE YOUR TEAM AND YOUR PRODUCTS?

We are inspired by what appears to be a common Scandinavian goal of creating good design for everyone, and aim to create well-made clothing and homewares that are affordable and accessible. The Ouur line is influenced by the cultures of both Scandinavia and Japan, as both of these regions have consistently focused on simplicity in design, making the best use of available and natural materials, and placing a high value on doing more with less. We spend a lot of time thinking about what to wear in rainy Portland – it shares a similar climate with the Scandinavian countries, so many of our warmer fabric choices and layered looks will parallel each other. We also look for manufacturers with a functional approach to their designs, making items that don't necessarily attract the most attention, but are made to last and have a practical use that seamlessly fits into the customer's lifestyle.

DO YOU HAVE ANY FAVOURITE PLACES WHERE YOU SEEK INSPIRATION?

I enjoy visiting Claus Meyer's Almanak restaurant in Copenhagen for traditional open-face sandwiches. His wife, Christina Meyer Bengtsson, is a talented graphic artist and has designed the interiors for each of his restaurants. The Louisiana Museum of Modern Art is also great for inspiration, along with the &tradition (p. 44) showroom on Paper Island.

WHO ARE YOUR FAVOURITE SCANDINAVIAN DESIGNERS?

I've been following the work of Niels Strøyer Christophersen and Driton Memisi and their team at the fairly young design studio Frama (p. 102), in Copenhagen. We're also keen on the product designs for the Menu design shop by Norm Architects (p. 172), as well as ceramics by Annemette Kissow.

MIA LINNMAN

Having previously worked for Ikea, Swedish designer Mia Linnman now writes the blog Solid Frog, has been included on Another Magazine's reading list and cited as a favourite of Triba Space. Her artwork is available through Saatchi Online.

HAVING GROWN UP SURROUNDED BY NORDIC DESIGN, WHAT DOES IT MEAN TO YOU TODAY?

I guess it has affected me in a really positive way: to be in environments full of light, pale colours and natural materials such as light wood, stone and leather. Scandinavian design has also given me a feeling of simplicity and an appreciation of quality.

YOUR BLOG HAS FOCUSED ATTENTION ON SCANDINAVIAN STYLE, BOTH IN TERMS OF FASHION AND LIFESTYLE. HOW DID IT START?

It actually started when I was working as an interior designer at Ikea. I felt that I had to collect inspiration somewhere and hopefully, in the long run, provide inspiration to others. It was also a kick to have a place to express what I liked – my style. I never really made any effort to attract readers – it just happened and suddenly I had followers, and that inspired me to keep on. Now I mainly post my own photos. It takes a lot more time, but it's much more fun and more personal.

WHO OR WHAT REPRESENTS NORDIC DESIGN TALENT TO YOU?

There are so many both new and established great Nordic design talents out there. I think Hay (p. 120) has really put Nordic design on the map when it comes to interior design. Product designer Pia Wallén also represents a true Nordic style. And also the Swedish style institution of Svenskt Tenn (p. 26). I also think that *Kinfolk* magazine (p. 238) is a Nordic design talent, because even though it's American, the focus is all about the Scandinavian lifestyle. I also admire AnnLouise Landelius and Paulina Liffner von Sydow of Little Liffner for their lovely style, making Scandinavian style a little bit more glamorous.

DO YOU IDENTIFY NORDIC DESIGN WITH A PARTICULAR PLACE?

The Louisiana Museum of Modern Art outside Copenhagen, Illums Bolighus, the Acne stores, Svenskt Tenn, Hay and Muuto (p. 156). Also the beautiful Ett Hem hotel in Stockholm.

DO YOU HAVE ANY FAVOURITE SCANDINAVIAN DESIGNERS?

The Danish classics are always nice. I like Thomas Sandell's style, and the work of multidisciplinary firm Claesson Koivisto Rune.

LOVE NORDIC

Half-Icelandic, half-English Samantha Denisdóttir is the interior designer behind the Love Nordic design blog. She studied at the National Design Academy, in Nottingham, and has worked for Danish furniture company BoConcept. Now living in Dorset, she designs interiors for hotels and private homes, while also writing for several magazines.

AS AN INTERIOR DESIGNER, WHAT IS YOUR TAKE ON NORDIC DESIGN?

I work with Nordic products every day. Scandinavian design is at the forefront of the interior-design industry. Its influence can be seen worldwide, especially now that the muted colours and simple, clean lines that characterize the Nordic look have filtered down into the high street.

DO YOU HAVE A FAVOURITE NORDIC DESIGNER, BOTH FROM THE PAST AND WORKING TODAY?

Hans J. Wegner is a favourite designer of mine. His work was one of the major influences on the Danish modern movement of the 1950s. It's no wonder that his pieces are still held in such high regard today. Norm Architects (p. 172), who are based in Copenhagen, create amazing interiors and their recent product designs for Menu have been utterly fantastic.

ABOVE Shelter, designed by Vipp

OPPOSITE, ABOVE Artists Michael Elmgreen, a Dane, and Ingar Dragset, from Norway, in their studio

OPPOSITE, BELOW Tableware collection for Noma, designed by Sonya Park

IS YOUR OWN WORK INFLUENCED BY SCANDINAVIAN DESIGN?

My main influence is my mother's home country of Iceland. Like many Icelandic designers, I am influenced by the nature, traditions and culture of this little dot in the North Atlantic Ocean. Icelandic design is characteristically Scandinavian, but has a raw beauty that resonates deeply with its landscape.

ARE THERE ANY PLACES YOU WOULD RECOMMEND TO VISITORS WANTING TO EXPERIENCE THE ICELANDIC DESIGN SCENE?

Reykjavik is an amazing place that is bursting with excellent restaurants. Sjavargrillið, in particular, is fantastic and super-cosy in winter; the sushi and lobster pasta is to die for! 101 Reykjavik is a cool design hotel, with a slick interior that epitomizes Icelandic design – in fact, the hotel doubles up as an art gallery. Even if you don't stay there, you must take a look and have a cocktail or two – in my opinion, the best in town. Of course, the natural world is a whole other story and not to be missed. The Blue Lagoon, erupting volcanos, icebergs and breeching whales – the list goes on! I have also spent a lot of time in Sweden: Stockholm is one of my favourite cities. Its grand architecture, beautiful people and breathtaking archipelago tick all the boxes for me. It must surely be one of the most ideal places to live. If you're in the neighbourhood, go to Lotta Agaton's shop in Rådmansgatan. She's an amazing interior stylist– prepare to be inspired! I am also desperate to go to Noma.

HAVE YOU COME ACROSS ANY NEW TALENT FROM SCANDINAVIA?

I am always coming across new talent for my online shop, Story North. A favourite designer is Ingibjorg Hanna Bjarnadóttir. She designed the 'Raven' hanger, which is quickly becoming a design classic. Another favourite is Thora Finnsdóttir, whose ceramic designs will be finding their way to my shop very soon.

PAUL SMITH

British fashion designer
Paul Smith's stripes are as
iconic and recognizable as the
most acclaimed items of Nordic
furniture design, so when the
two came together in a pair of
recent projects, it was a match
made in heaven.

To mark the 100th anniversary of Danish
furniture designer Hans J. Wegner's birth,
Smith teamed up with Carl Hansen & Son, a
leading Danish furniture company for over one
hundred years, and US textile firm Maharam
to produce a limited-edition furniture collection.
The project, 'Paul Smith Celebrates Wegner',
revisited some of Wegner's most iconic designs,
including 'Wishbone' (1949), 'Wing' (1960) and
'Shell' (1963), which were covered by two new
patterns designed by Smith, 'Big Stripe' and
'Stripes', in varying colourways. The collection
debuted at the Paul Smith shop and the Carl
Hansen & Son showroom in Milan during the
2014 Salone del Mobile, with a touring exhibition
travelling to Tokyo, New York and London.

Two years earlier, Smith had joined forces
with Maharam, textile manufacturer Kvadrat,
based in Ebeltoft, Denmark, and another iconic
Danish furniture brand – Republic of Fritz Hansen
(p. 30) – to produce a new textile, 'Point'. The
fabric design was produced in seven different
patterns, in eleven colourways, and to celebrate
its launch, it was used to cover a range of Fritz
Hansen's classic chair designs, including Arne
Jacobsen's chair designs 'Egg' and 'Swan', both
from 1958, and 'Grand Prix' from 1957, and Poul
Kjærholm's 'PK22' chair from 1956. The chairs
were exhibited in 2012 at the Republic of Fritz
Hansen's flagship store in London.

ABOVE Paul Smith with a 'Swan' chair, originally
designed by Arne Jacobsen

OPPOSITE 'Egg' and 'Swan' chairs, covered
in 'Point'

SKANDIUM

British company Skandium was founded in 1999 by three Scandinavians – Magnus Englund, Christina Schmidt and Christopher Seidenfaden – and is now one of the most prominent retailers of Scandinavian furniture in the UK. The managing director Magnus Englund has a background in fashion retail and is the author of two bestselling books on Scandinavian design.

HOW DO YOU SEE SCANDINAVIAN DESIGN INFLUENCING THE GLOBAL DESIGN SCENE, AND VICE VERSA?

In my world, Scandinavia, Italy, the US, Britain and Germany rule design. But I think design with a national identity is becoming less relevant in a globalized world, with manufacturing often physically removed from the design process. What Scandinavian designers bring is more a way of working, in which simplicity is regarded as a virtue.

WHAT SCANDINAVIAN DESIGNER DO YOU ADMIRE MOST IN TERMS OF TALENT AND VERSATILITY?

Within the 'golden age' of Scandinavian design, I regard Tapio Wirkkala as perhaps the most talented. His work covers so many aspects, everything from the design of small household objects to city planning, and had such integrity. I'm also a big collector of Stig Lindberg's ceramics, because they have wit and warmth.

HAVE ANY EXPERIENCES INFLUENCED YOU PARTICULARLY IN YOUR CAREER?

Spending time in Finland during the centenary year of Alvar Aalto's birth really opened up my eyes to Finnish modernism. Working for Paul Smith (p. 244) was an excellent school in retailing for me. His attention to detail is amazing, and he showed me that you don't have to be nasty to be successful.

WHAT INSPIRES YOU MOST ABOUT SCANDINAVIAN ARCHITECTURE AND DESIGN?

I can find pleasure in the most mundane qualities of buildings from the last century, such as door handles, light fittings and handrails. Today those things all look the same, but back then they really went for quality and unique designs for each new building. I even like my old school building!

IS THERE A PARTICULAR DESIGN HUB FOR THE NEW NORDIC DESIGN?

Denmark is really the place where it's happening right now, there's been a big shift from Stockholm to Copenhagen over the last few years. Previously, Danish designers were caught like rabbits in the headlights by the heavy heritage of the mid-twentieth-century masters, but a new generation has managed to break away from all that and design for today, and the success has been remarkable.

ALLAN TORP

Founder and editor-in-chief of the blog collective Bungalow 5, Allan Torp escaped the fashion industry to focus on interiors. He works for a range of Danish design brands, including Gubi (p. 112), and writes for interiors magazines. He also set up the Bloggers Tour, showcasing nine of the most influential design bloggers in Europe.

WHAT IS THE DIFFERENCE BETWEEN THE NEW TALENTS OF TODAY AND THE DESIGNERS OF THE PAST?
More and more new designers get the recognition they deserve at international fairs and by the press, both indicators that they are heading in the right direction. It is safe to say that the cultural heritage that has permeated Scandinavian design is still relevant today, although in a more improved and complex way than before. Modern Scandinavian design is developing – fast! The new generation of designers have taken the combination of influences from their surroundings and their unique national customs and made them their own. Global success is achieved through the promotion of one's inheritance – something they really understand.

ABOVE Bungalow 5 is part of the 'Bloggers Tour', nine bloggers from nine different European countries

I don't have just one, I have many. I love Norm
Architects (p. 172), who have taken design objects
to new level; their timelessness is something else.
And Afteroom – although they were originally
from Taiwan, they now work from their studio in
Stockholm. Their sense of simplicity and honesty
is remarkable. I love it when Scandinavians
get together with people from other countries,
combining their talents and cultural references but
still keeping it Scandinavian – which is the case
with the Danish-Italian duo GamFratesi and the
Swedish-Italian group Note Design.

**ARE YOU INFLUENCED BY ANY OTHER
SCANDINAVIAN PLATFORM, IN TERMS
OF NORDIC DESIGN?**

I have always looked to the best international
design blogs, one being Emmas Designblogg, by the
Swedish blogger Em. She has an amazing sense of
aesthetics that I really love. Today she is also a good
friend, and we work together closely on a number
of projects. I also look to other internationally
known blogs, such as Yatzer and Dezeen. They
convey design in a very interesting way, and have
a unique take on how to be commercial without
it compromising the essence of the blog.

**DO YOU HAVE ANY SECRET PLACES IN
SCANDINAVIA THAT YOU WILL SHARE?**

I have lived in Copenhagen my entire life – even
though it is small, compared to other capitals in the
world, it still has its perks. I enjoy walking instead
of biking or taking public transport – you can walk
pretty much anywhere in an hour. I love the culture
of the different areas of Copenhagen. Vesterbro is
very creative and artsy, and there are many great
coffee houses and restaurants around Istedgade
and the meatpacking district (Kødbyen). Nørrebro
is very diverse culturally, and you find more and
more buildings worth seeing, such as Superkilen,
a new urban open space. Østerbro is great for its
historical buildings, and I love walking around the
star fortress, Kastellet, following the harbour into
the city with sites like the new opera house and

the playhouse. And you cannot visit Copenhagen
without going to the great restaurants, like Höst or
Geranium, seeing sights such Grundtvig's Church
and the Ny Carlsberg Glyptoteket, and shopping
at Hay (p. 120) or Stilleben.

**WHO DO YOU SEE AMONG THE
EMERGING TALENTS OF THE NEW
NORDIC DESIGN?**

A few come to mind. Christina Liljenberg
Halstrøm has been a household name in the
design world for a few years and was quickly
snapped up by Trip Trap, who got her 'Georg'
collection into production. Very new to the
scene are Straight Lines and Hanna Dalrot,
both have great talent and potential.

VERONICA MIKE SOLHEIM

Blogger Veronica Mike Solheim is editor-in-chief at Anti, an award-winning creative agency, based in Oslo, with an international client base in Tokyo, Paris and New York, and beyond. Her blog, World of Mike, won the 2013 Blogger of the Year award in Norway.

HOW DO YOU SEE NORDIC DESIGN TODAY?

For me, the new Nordic design, and in particular Norwegian design, has a splendid balance between design and function. I could stress the clean lines and simplicity, but there is so much more to it than that. It has a rich cultural history – the designs we see now are a development of what our ancestors did hundreds of years ago, which makes them all the more authentic. It's intriguing and honest, and has a certain serenity to it.

DO YOU HAVE ANY FAVOURITE NORWEGIAN DESIGNERS?

I love the skill of craftsmanship and authentic brand stories, which we often find in Scandinavian design. Right now I'm really fond of the emerging duo Hunting & Narud (p. 134) – their mix of materials is very beautiful and uniquely done. I love the functionality of Muuto (p. 156), I absolutely adore Hay (p. 120), and I'm obsessed with Trond Svendgård's 'Snowball' lamp.

WHAT HAS INFLUENCED YOU MOST IN YOUR CAREER?

I work for the Norwegian design company Anti, which stands for 'a new type of interference' – you might call it our philosophy. We are always looking for new ways to communicate. I'm particularly drawn to how specific words and visual techniques can tell stories. The combination of authenticity and interference is something that's always influenced me – it's what fascinates me about other people's work and what I aim for in my own.

WHAT ARE YOUR FAVOURITE PLACES OF INSPIRATION IN SCANDINAVIA, AND ESPECIALLY IN NORWAY?

I've lived in Norway my whole life and grew up on the west coast, where the natural world is a magnificent discovery and such an inspiration for any designer, myself included. My favourite city is definitely Copenhagen, with all its restaurants and the constant appearance of new designers. Oslo, where I live now, is experiencing a very interesting transformation. A good example is YME, a concept store *Frame* magazine described as the 'jewel in the crown' of the newly refurbished Paleet Mall in the centre of Oslo. It is a wonderful store, a meeting place for fashion, art and design enthusiasts, and is a breath of fresh air for Oslo residents.

HAVE YOU COME ACROSS ANY NEW DESIGN TALENT FROM SCANDINAVIA?

Through my work at Anti I've spent the last ten months hunting talent in this small country. I want to highlight Maria Bjørlykke, Reiulf Ramstad Architects, Kråkvik & D'Orazio and Erik Friis Reitan – they all represent Scandinavian design, while maintaining a close connection with their Norwegian cultural heritage.

ILSE CRAWFORD

Although based in London, designer Ilse Crawford's Nordic connections are strong. Her mother is Danish (from the Faroe Islands), and Crawford herself, together with her team at Studioilse, has designed many interiors across Scandinavia, for such clients as Stockholm hotel Ett Hem and The Apartment, as well as a range of products for Danish jewelry brand Georg Jensen.

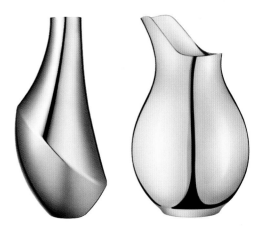

Having worked in an architectural firm and as a design journalist, she was then, aged twenty-seven, appointed the first editor of the UK edition of *Elle Decoration*. Later she worked as the vice president of Donna Karan Home in New York, before forming her own studio. Among her many projects are the interiors for Soho House New York and Duddell's restaurant in Hong Kong (2013), as well as a capsule range for Ikea, and she was invited, as the guest of honour, to curate an exhibition (*Question Time...*) in the entrance hall of the 2015 Stockholm Furniture Fair.

Drawing on her Scandinavian background in the choice of furniture and simple style, Crawford's interiors are comfortable and welcoming, In Scandinavia, projects include the interiors for Mathias Dahlgren's restaurants in the Stockholm Grand Hôtel, lighting for Swedish lighting brand Wästberg, as well as brand identity and the interiors for luxury hotel Ett Hem, also in Stockholm, and a temporary interior design for The Apartment (p. 206), which included turning the kitchen into a pop-up restaurant. Her projects extend outside the

Nordic countries: she is also the founder of the Department of Man and Wellbeing at the Design Academy Eindhoven, in the Netherlands, and designed an installation for VitraHaus, in Weil-am-Rhein, Germany.

Crawford has written and spoken passionately about her belief that interiors should be welcoming, comfortable spaces, that make sense for everyday life. In that respect, the design philosophy of this half-Danish, half-Canadian designer based in London is perfectly attuned to the aesthetics of the New Nordic Design.

ABOVE 'Ilse Collection' for Georg Jensen, 2012

OPPOSITE Ett Hem, Stockholm, 2012

ON P. 254 Nathan Williams, of Kinfolk

ON P. 256 'Pull' lamp, designed by WhatsWhat for Muuto

DIRECTORY

&tradition [44]
andtradition.com

Aalto + Aalto [48]
aaltoaalto.com

Camilla Akersveen [52]
camillaakersveen.no

Arabia [16]
arabia.fi

Artek [20]
artek.fi

John Astbury [56]
johnastbury.com

Bare Møbler [60]
baremobler.no

Beller [64]
beller.no

Berns Hotel [68]
berns.se/hotel

Birger1962 [72]
birger1962.com

Emilia
Borgthorsdóttir [76]
emiliaborgthor.com

Dominique
Browning [230]
domiquebrowning.com
slowlovelife.com

byKATO [80]
bykato.com

By Lassen [84]
bylassen.com

Ilse Crawford [252]
studioilse.com

Amanda Dameron [228]
dwell.com

Dysthe Design [18]
dysthedesign.no

Olafur Eliasson [88]
olafureliasson.net

David Ericsson [92]
davidericsson.se
dmoch.se

Everything Elevated [94]
everything-elevated.com

Færid [98]
faerid.com

Frama [102]
framacph.com

Futudesign [106]
futudesign.com

Garbo Interiors [110]
garbointeriors.com

Gubi [112]
gubi.dk

Sigurdur Gustafsson [40]
scandinaviandesign.com

Guðný
Hafsteinsdóttir [116]
gudnyhaf.is

Hay [120]
hay.dk

Hotel sp34 [126]
brochner-hotels.dk

HTL Stockholm [130]
htlhotels.com

Hunting & Narud [134]
huntingandnarud.com

Finn Juhl [24]
finnjuhl.com

Källemo [28]
kallemo.se

Kinfolk [238]
ouurcollection.com
kinfolk.com

Kneip [136]
kneip.com

Krads [138]
krads.info

Joanna Laajisto [142]
joannalaajisto.com

Mia Linnman [240]
mialinnman.blogspot.com

Lith Lith Lundin [146]
lithlithlundin.se

Love Nordic [242]
lovenordic.co.uk
storynorth.com

Cecilie Manz [150]
ceciliemanz.com

Miss Clara [154]
missclarahotel.com

Muuto [156]
muuto.com

Ditte Buus Nielsen [162]
dittebuus.com

Nikari [164]
nikari.fi

Nordic Design [234]
nordicdesign.ca

Normann
Copenhagen [168]
normann-copenhagen.com

Norm Architects [172]
normcph.com

Oaxen Krog [176]
oaxen.com

Objecthood [180]
objecthood.se

Caroline Olsson [182]
carolineolsson.no

Republic of
Fritz Hansen [30]
fritzhansen.com

Timo Ripatti [184]
studioripatti.fi

Eva Schildt [188]
evaschildt.se

Skandium [246]
skandium.com

Paul Smith [244]
paulsmithcelebrateswegner.com

Snickeriet [190]
snickeriet.com

Martin Solem [192]
martinsolem.com

Veronica Mike
Solheim [250]
worldofmike.no

Space Copenhagen [194]
spacecph.dk

Spark Design Space [198]
sparkdesignspace.com

Studio Fem [202]
studiofem.dk

Svenskt Tenn [26]
svenskttenn.se

Swedese [36]
swedese.com

The Apartment [206]
theapartment.dk

Anna Thórunn [210]
annathorunn.is

Allan Torp [248]
bungalow5.dk

Atle Tveit [214]
atletveitdesign.no

Bjørn
Van den Berg [218]
bjornvandenberg.no

Susanna Vento [233]
susannavento.fi
pikkuvarpunen.blogspot.co.uk

Vera & Kyte [222]
vera-kyte.com

PHOTO CREDITS

All illustrations are provided courtesy of the designer, architect or manufacturer, unless otherwise noted below.